PRAISE FOR
CHOOSE YOUR STORY, CHANGE YOUR LIFE

"As a therapist, I know how powerful the stories we create about ourselves can be. *Choose Your Story, Change Your Life* teaches us how to change our narrative. It's a must-read for anyone who wants to create a different path for themselves."

—Amy Morin,
Bestselling author of
13 Things Mentally Strong People Don't Do

"I am successful because years ago, I took control of my own story. *Choose Your Story, Change Your Life* will show you how to create a powerful story for yourself that inspires and engages others from the inside out."

—Ryan Serhant,
Founder of SERHANT., bestselling
author of *Big Money Energy*, Bravo TV Star

"In *Choose Your Story, Change Your Life*, Kindra Hall outlines a profound yet simple approach to tapping into the power of your inner voice. Through her guidance, you will deepen your connection within and become a catalyst for change."

—Gabby Bernstein,
#1 *New York Times* bestselling
author of *The Universe Has Your Back*

"If you've ever sensed that the thing holding you back from achieving greatness isn't entirely an outside obstacle—that maybe there's something inside of you keeping you tethered to where you are—you're not wrong. In *Choose Your Story, Change Your Life*, Kindra Hall takes the power of storytelling to a whole new place—*inside* our own minds—and shows how the key to success has been within us all along."

—Dave Hollis,
New York Times bestselling
author of *Get Out of Your Own Way*

"Kindra Hall is a master storyteller and knows how to tap into the power that stories have to inspire and transform. In *Choose Your Story, Change Your Life*, she shows us how to spot the hidden stories behind our behaviors and how to write all-new scripts for any part of our lives."

—Mel Robbins,
International bestselling author of *The 5 Second Rule*

"When I look back on my life and the risks I've taken, so many of them were possible because I chose to tell myself stories that encouraged me to fearlessly take the next step. *Choose Your Story, Change Your Life* is the missing piece for anyone who has felt stuck and isn't exactly sure why. Look no further than the stories you're choosing to tell yourself."

—Rebecca Minkoff,
Founder of the Rebecca Minkoff global brand, author of *Fearless*

"*Choose Your Story, Change Your Life* will leave you asking yourself, 'What story am I telling myself here, and does it serve me?' A radical approach to self-talk and personal perspective, Kindra Hall's digestible storytelling process teaches you how to find, edit, and ultimately use the stories you already have inside of you to redefine and up-level your finances, relationships, business, and life."

—Patrice Washington,
Award-winning host of the *Redefining Wealth* podcast

"My entire business is focused on helping people achieve their physical health goals, and I see the lessons in *Choose Your Story, Change Your Life* play out in real time every single day. People who choose to tell themselves stories that fuel their motivation and belief in what they're capable of are far more likely to achieve their health goals than those who don't. This book will change lives."

—Autumn Calabrese,
Fitness expert, bestselling author of *Lose Weight Like Crazy Even if You Have a Crazy Life*, creator of Ultimate Portion Fix

KINDRA HALL

CHOOSE YOUR
STORY,
CHANGE YOUR
LIFE

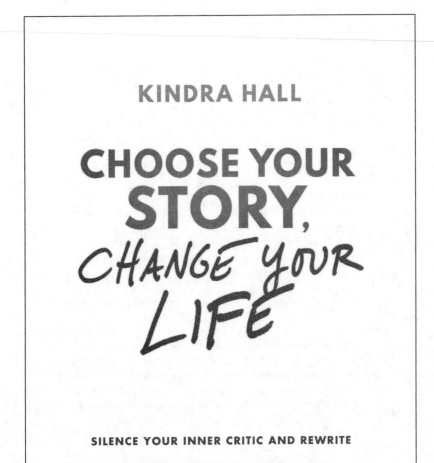

SILENCE YOUR INNER CRITIC AND REWRITE

YOUR LIFE FROM THE INSIDE OUT

HarperCollins
LEADERSHIP

AN IMPRINT OF HarperCollins

Published by HarperCollins Leadership,
an imprint of HarperCollins Focus LLC.

Any internet addresses, phone numbers, or company or product information printed in this book are offered as a resource and are not intended in any way to be or to imply an endorsement by HarperCollins Leadership, nor does HarperCollins Leadership vouch for the existence, content, or services of these sites, phone numbers, companies, or products beyond the life of this book.

ISBN 978-1-4002-2848-5 (TP)
ISBN 978-1-4002-2841-6 (eBook)
ISBN 978-1-4002-2840-9 (HC)

Library of Congress Control Number: 2021949040

Printed in the United States of America
23 24 25 26 27 LBC 5 4 3 2 1

This book is for the storyteller that lives within you.
May the stories you choose to tell be good ones.

CONTENTS

PART III: HACKING YOUR ESSENTIAL STORIES
TALES OF TRANSFORMATION

INTRODUCTION

The Real Yellow Brick Road

It was Thanksgiving weekend. Six thousand miles away, people were eating turkey and mashed potatoes, sharing what they were grateful for, and passing out on couches with the dull roar of football playing in the background.

I was doing none of those things, because I was in . . . Slovenia.

I'll be honest, "I'm in Slovenia" is not necessarily something I ever imagined I would say, but I was there to speak at a marketing conference about storytelling, and my husband, Michael, and I decided to turn a work trip into a brief vacation.

Let me pause for a moment to say, if you feel like you've heard this story before, it's because those are the opening lines of *Stories That Stick,* my book about the power of storytelling in business. These were the moments right before I heard the greatest sales story of my life about a bottle of cologne and before I walked out of that Slovenian shop with my husband wanting to launch his own cologne empire.

And while I love that story . . . I didn't tell you the whole thing.

Despite a deal that Michael and I had made not to buy anything on our vacation (not the best deal, looking back), I had been lured into the shop with the cologne in the first place by a contraband pair of shoes.

These were not just any shoes; they were a pair of sparkly, glittery shoes. A pair whose sequins were perfectly positioned to catch the light in the window and the eye of someone like me.

This is the part of the story I haven't told. A story of a woman who has always been a sucker for sparkly shoes and one who grew up fascinated with a different story—one about a girl named Dorothy, her ruby slippers, an emerald city, and a yellow brick road to take you there.

That is where *this* story begins.

With a girl who loved all things *Wizard of Oz*.

I spent much of my childhood as Dorothy. I had the light-blue checkered dress. I had a pair of black patent shoes that my mother soaked in glue and covered in red glitter. I had a small, brown stuffed dog whom I called Toto (even though her name was Sheila) and carried around in a basket that was supposed to be for the toilet paper in the bathroom.

For four consecutive Halloweens, I was Dorothy. One year I made my family join in; Dad was the Tin Man, Mom was the Scarecrow, little brother was the Lion, and my sister was a Care Bear (we ran out of Oz costumes). Every year I wore the same Dorothy dress. Every year my Dorothy got a little more inappropriate as I grew and the dress didn't. Every year for Christmas we made ornaments to give as gifts to friends, family, and our teachers at school. My brother made Christmas trees; my sister made candy canes. I made Dorothys. And while I never quite perfected my yellow-brick-road skip, I could sing every word of "Over the Rainbow" and even nailed the instrumental "ree-ii-deet-dee-dee-dee-dee-dee" portion of the "We're Off to See the Wizard" number every time.

When I look back, my obsession with *The Wizard of Oz* centered on three things. The ruby slippers, yes. That one was obvious. But (almost) equally fascinating were the Emerald City and the yellow brick road that could take you to it.

Even as a child, I knew that if the Emerald City was a place where a horse could be any color, then it was a place where I could be any*thing*. Now, grown-up me understands the Emerald City as a version of self-actualization, or happiness, or success. It's the place we all wish and work for in all areas of life. In the Emerald City, we've reached our potential. We have meaningful relationships, our bodies are healthy, and financial abundance is all around. Decorating the walls of the Emerald City are framed vision boards come true and lists of New Year's resolutions achieved. The Emerald City is the manifestation of your version of success, and it is absolutely worth enduring a few apple-throwing trees and mutated monkey attacks.

Of course, to get to the Emerald City, you needed a yellow brick road, and my young Dorothy self was determined to find it. Everywhere I went, I searched for signs of the yellow brick road. I spent late afternoons standing alone at the top of the hill overlooking our sweeping Minnesota backyard hoping to catch a glimpse of a rogue yellow brick. As the sun set and the world around me turned that unique Midwest-summer shade of gold, I carefully scanned the scene for evidence of a twisting yellow path.

It seemed so easy. So straightforward. Find the yellow brick road, follow it in an otherworldly pair of heels, find the Emerald City. Live happily ever after. I didn't know the word *destiny*. I couldn't articulate the concept of fulfillment. But that didn't stop me from looking for the path that would get me there; the road that could take me to my own personal Emerald City.

One early birthday, I received the *best* gift my Dorothy heart could ask for: two tickets to a community theater production of *The Wizard of Oz*. I didn't even know what theater *was*, but I knew it meant I was going to *see* Dorothy. I knew it meant going to see Toto and Glinda and the munchkins. I was *going* to Oz. And I trembled with excitement when I realized I was finally going to see the yellow brick road.

When the day of the play finally arrived, I put on my too-short Dorothy dress and my black shoes that left a trail of red glitter everywhere I walked, then clicked my heels and I was ready. I remember sitting in the theater before the show. It was packed with people and a growing murmur of excitement—community theater at its finest. My mother and I were on the aisle about twelve rows from the stage and I was talking to her. Nonstop. Very loudly. I had many questions. Will the tornado hurt us? What do flying monkeys eat? Is that man in front of us with no hair a munchkin? She answered all of them, she always did, but in a hushed tone. Just as I was about to inquire where I could get my own floating bubble, the room went dark, the curtains opened, and the show began.

It was *magic*.

I saw Auntie Em and Uncle Henry. Miss Gulch rode in on her bike (almost right into the barn that was plywood painted by high school kids, but Uncle Henry grabbed her bike basket just in time). Toto was there and only peed on the stage once. I mouthed along to every word of "Over the Rainbow." I cowered in my seat as the tech crew banged on pieces of metal backstage and the light crew flashed the lights to simulate a tornado. I nodded in agreement with Dorothy when she stated she was no longer in Kansas. I adored the children dressed as munchkins and even the munchkin adults who duck-walked around trying to fit the part. When Glinda arrived in her billowing pink prom dress and crown (rolled out on a platform with wheels by the stage crew dressed in all black and blowing bubbles), I thought I had died and gone to heaven. When the green woman in a witch hat with an evil cackle took the stage in a sad little puff of paprika, I hid my face until she was gone.

The moment Dorothy slipped her feet into the most sparkly, glittery pair of red slippers I'd ever seen, I gasped aloud. They were real rubies. I knew it. It was *all* real. I sat quietly in my seat, mesmerized.

And then came the moment I'd waited for.

Glinda pointed her wand to the floor of the stage and said in a voice as sweet as the curls in my pigtails, "Follow the yellow brick road."

The munchkins repeated the sentiment. "Follow the yellow brick road."

Everyone on the stage was pointing to the floor chanting, "Follow the yellow brick road."

And there was *nothing* there.

No bricks. No stones. No paint. No brick-shaped stickers. Not even a few scraps of yellow and orange construction paper. Nothing that even *resembled* a yellow brick road. I frantically looked around the theater—to the people sitting around me, to the munchkin-man sitting in front of me, to my mother, who'd brought me there in the first place. Was no one going to say anything? Did no one else see something very, *very* wrong with this picture? I knew I had to do something.

I stood up in my chair and shouted in my loudest outside voice: *"There is no yellow brick road!"*

Everything stopped. The actors fell silent. The audience turned.

Everyone in the theater stared at the three-foot-tall Dorothy in a blue-checkered miniskirt, covered in intermittent red glitter, holding a stuffed dog dangling from a rope in one hand and pointing angrily at the stage with the other.

I would venture to guess you've been here before.

You know what you want and where you want to go. You might even know how to get there. You've worked on yourself. You've meditated. You've written affirmations, set goals, and focused on positive thinking. You've worked with an executive coach, streamlined your productivity. You know your Enneagram, your Myers-Briggs personality type. Maybe you've talked to a therapist or a healer. You get enough sleep, drink enough water, and exercise. Or maybe you've done none of the above, preferring to listen to podcasts by great thinkers and read the classic personal development books. No matter your method, no one would ever say you haven't put in the work to reach the Emerald City.

And yet, you just can't seem to get there.

And then, as if to add insult to injury, all around you are people—friends, colleagues, Instagram influencers—skipping and dancing down a phantom path. Some of them even move their arm in an exaggerated gesture inviting you to "follow the yellow brick road." And even though they're pointing at something that isn't there, *you* feel like the crazy person.

After the initial shock of the outburst, the play continued while my mother placed a graceful hand on my shoulder and helped me back into my seat. I was appalled by the injustice. The tickets may have been a gift, but I wanted my money back. How was anyone supposed to get to the Emerald City if no one would ever actually show the road? Why keep the road a secret?! I've never been one for conspiracy theories but even I knew something was up.

My mother leaned over to whisper that it was okay. Everything would be okay.

I whispered back, at a child's volume and with genuine concern: "If there was no yellow brick road, how do Dorothys ever meet the wizard?"

There, in a dark theater, while mediocre actors made their way down a nonexistent road, my mother leaned over and spoke in the way that only mothers can. "Sweet Kindra. Most Dorothys have to find their *own* way to the Emerald City. Real-life Dorothys *create* the yellow brick road." She then redirected my attention toward the stage where a man flopped around the set complaining about a lack of straw and the need for a brain.

Decades of searching later, I am certain of a few things. First, yes, the Emerald City is real—it is as unique and individualized as our fingerprints, the snowflakes that blanket Central Park in the winter, and the freckle-pattern on my daughter's face after just a minute in the sun, but it is real.

And yes, you need a yellow brick road to get you there.

Fortunately, the yellow brick road is also real. But, as my mother said, it's not just sitting around, waiting to be found.

You have to build it.

Day by day. Choice by choice. Action by action. Brick by golden brick.

And here's the most important piece.

Those bricks aren't actually made of gold (good news for those of us not rolling in precious metals). They are made of something far more valuable and much more prevalent—literally the most abundant resource in the world. You have, at your immediate disposal, *more* of this material than you could ever need. You have so much that you could build a yellow brick road to one Emerald City, live there for a while, develop it, and then decide to relocate to a different Emerald City on the other side of the country, build a yellow brick road to get there, and *still* have enough material left over to do it again. Not only that, for every day that goes by, more of the raw material is created. All you have to do is use it.

That yellow brick road—*your* yellow brick road—the one responsible for leading you to the destiny *you* desire, is composed entirely of the *stories you tell yourself.*

The good news is that you are a great storyteller. Or if not a great one, then at least one who is prolific.

The bad news is that all stories are not created equal.

Choosing the right stories is the only way to create the road to the future you desire.

Yes. You're not in Kansas anymore.

INTRODUCING THE WORLD'S MOST PROLIFIC STORYTELLER . . . *YOU*

Whether you realize it or not, right now, you're telling yourself a story.

I don't mean story like the kind you tell customers about how great your company is. Or the one you tell your kids that starts *when I was your age.* Or even that one you tell friends at dinner about that time a smart, grown woman and a friendly older gentleman complimented your shoes at the mall and during your innocent exchange he somehow was able to get your date of birth and phone number and your friends, shocked, double-checked to make sure you didn't also hand over your Social Security number. Those may be great, albeit embarrassing, stories but they're not the stories of this book. They're not the stories that are changing your life even as you read this.

I'm talking about the stories you tell *yourself*.

THE INVISIBLE STORIES THAT CREATE YOUR LIFE

These "self-stories" are different. For the most part, they're invisible to you. You keep telling them, but you don't realize you're doing it. They're a habit. They are as invisible to you as your accent or the scent of your home. They're in your line of vision, you just don't see them. Not really.

That being said, you've almost certainly glimpsed your self-stories. You may have caught sight of one because you said it aloud—to a partner, a friend, a family member. Like the time when I had just started dating my husband and he suggested we join a bunch of our friends on a skiing trip. I said no because I hated skiing. He asked me when I skied last, and I told him I skied once, in fourth grade, and then told him the whole story about how terrible it was as if a slightly unpleasant ski experience from two and a half decades earlier was justification to never try it again.

Perhaps you've seen a self-story run by, out of the corner of your subconscious eye, like when you're nervous or about to do something new. Self-stories get particularly aggressive anytime you feel that impulse to make a more intentional foray toward your Emerald City like when you've decided to take a risk, or act boldly, or do something outside your comfort zone. But more often—*most* often—you tell these stories to yourself, inside your head, where it's dark and no one, not even you, can see what's really happening.

But just because you usually can't see them doesn't mean they aren't there.

These self-stories exist.

And it is entirely possible you've gone most of your life without realizing that each day, all day, you are whispering a near-steady stream of them into your own ear.

You might not consider yourself a storyteller, yet you are. Evolution wired it right into you. It's a legacy from your ancient ancestors who used stories to survive, to create meaning, and to thrive.

The remarkable thing about this self-storytelling, however, is not that it exists—the truth is both far weirder and more wonderful. The crazy thing about self-stories is that *they actually become your life.* Your self-stories become true. They are an ongoing, self-fulfilling prophecy.

That, above all, is the most amazing part: *we become our stories.*

The stories you tell yourself *are* your yellow brick road. They determine the way you think and feel. They influence how you act and which way you go. The stories you tell yourself are deeply powerful predictors of *what you are becoming and what your life will be.*

But as I've said, not all self-stories are created equal.

Not all self-stories are good for you.

In those moments when you feel lost or behind or inadequate or like you'll never get to where you know you can be, and you're just so tired of trying, that's a sure sign that your self-stories have taken you on a path back into the dark forest, through some poppy fields, and locked you in a witch's tower instead of leading you to the Emerald City.

That's the bad news.

The good news is, you have the power to change them.

What happens when you change the stories you tell yourself?

What happens when you choose better ones?

You change your life.

CHOOSE YOUR STORY, CHANGE YOUR LIFE

It can be unsettling to realize that you have an entire world of almost invisible storytelling going on inside you. And perhaps even a little scary to discover that those stories are determining how your life unfolds. But beyond that uncertainty is a powerful idea: that you can take control of those stories, and through them, take control of your *life*.

I've seen it happen. I've watched people's lives transform simply by changing the stories they tell themselves and choosing better ones. And I'll admit, there were times I stared in disbelief as they shared their transformation and progress. How they could go from being so blocked to suddenly breaking through—all because of the stories they chose to put on repeat. It was as magical as the first time I saw Dorothy click her heels together and realize that, all that time, she had the power within her.

That power is within you. And this book is your pair of ruby slippers. In the pages ahead, you'll learn:

- What your self-stories are, where they come from, and why you have them.
- How to catch your inner storyteller in the act and identify the stories holding you back.
- How to choose better stories (don't worry, you have them) and effectively install them into the forefront of your mind so they are always the go-to when it comes to your self-talk.
- How this self-storytelling approach works in key areas to instill within you the two ingredients of every well-lived life: hope and *power*.

It's a positive, empowering journey. Along the way, you'll see how others have changed their lives for the better, too, including the story of:

- Roberta, the first-time entrepreneur who used a story from her previous job to help reach her business goals.
- Julia, who uncovered the stories that were sabotaging her relationship, and her journey back to love.
- Sam, who used storytelling to rediscover his purpose at work.
- Cori, who found her story triggers and found her way back to a healthy lifestyle.
- And there are many more stories and self-storytelling resources at www.chooseyourstorychangeyourlife.com/resources.

They all learned to carefully curate their stories and lay a direct path, brick by brick, story by story, to the life they've always wanted.

And you'll get all the tools you need to do the very same thing.

Which means: *you are about to become the author of your own life.*

THE STORY OF YOUR LIFE

This book is about changing the story of your life by changing the voice in your head. How to change the way you are on the *inside* to change the *outside*. If you're dissatisfied with your financial life, for example, there's a story there, mostly hidden, that needs rewriting. Not happy with your romantic life? There's a story there, too. Your health? Yep. Story.

The moment you identify one of those self-stories and drag it into the light of day is the moment that change begins. It's the moment when you realize the yellow brick road is yours to build. Choose your stories poorly, and the road will lead you toward where you've always gone. It's a circular road that revisits the same places: the same income, the same relationship problems, the same insecurities, the same disappointments.

Choose your stories wisely, and you will build a path to achieving your greatness. It's the road of prosperity. The one where you find true connection in love and relationships. It's the road that will carry you to develop the confidence to thrive in work and business. Where you find abundance in all areas of life.

Choose Your Story, Change Your Life is about uncovering the truth of how you created the life you have, and the clear steps you can take to create the one you *want*. All the tools you need to rewrite your stories lie ahead, along with the tales of people like you who have done it.

The ideas and stories ahead will challenge what you think you know about how your life is created and how change happens. You might be surprised at what you find—at what stories have been dictating your path and how you didn't even realize it. In some respects, what I am about to teach you is painfully simple, almost embarrassingly so at times. Don't let that simplicity deceive you. Rather than lead you to underestimate what is possible, it should inspire you to reimagine your life in a way you never have before and give you the faith to know that life is attainable.

———————

One of my favorite parts of *The Wizard of Oz* was the very end when Glinda arrives, tells Dorothy and her fellow travelers that Dorothy had always had the power within her. The Scarecrow speaks accusingly to the good witch, asking, "Then why didn't you tell her before?"

Glinda responds, "Because she wouldn't have believed me. She had to learn it for herself."

There is no yellow brick road just waiting to be found—at least not one that's just on the outskirts of town with an overgrown sign or one that starts at the second turn of the roundabout—but you, too, have the power within you. And I hope by the end of our time together, like Dorothy, you'll have discovered it.

Whether you are a sucker for sparkly shoes or not, your great story starts here.

PART I

YOU BECOME YOUR STORY

The Powerful Stories Within You

WIRED FOR STORY

Where Your Self-Stories Come From

Even when the body goes to sleep, the
mind stays up all night, telling itself stories.

—JONATHAN GOTTSCHALL

Meet Mike.

You're going to meet many people throughout this book and Mike is a great place to start because he is simply a great guy. He's funny, curious, charismatic, and loyal. He's the father of three, a dedicated husband, and hard worker. He is always working—on the weekends he works in the yard and during the week he commutes an hour each way to the office where he worked as a program director for a large nonprofit. He's good at his job and he's been rising through the ranks as a result. And while he doesn't love the commute (especially not in the winter) and he really doesn't love the pay (a fraction of what his friends who went the corporate route make), and sometimes he wonders if the stress and intensity of the job are digging him an early grave (his programs are primarily focused on the perpetrators and victims of domestic abuse) and even though, if he were totally honest, he'd considered finding something better since almost as soon as he'd started . . . he stayed. It was a good, stable job. He was able to provide a good (not grand, but good) life for his family and that was good enough. Wasn't it?

Or was it?

And then one day, he got his answer.

Mike had been assigned a new supervisor who, for whatever reason, really didn't like Mike. The supervisor sabotaged Mike's projects, reallocated his funding, and scrambled his well-established team. No matter how hard Mike worked, no matter what great ideas or initiatives he put out, the supervisor questioned Mike's decisions, undermined what authority Mike had, and publicly criticized his work. When the time came for his annual review, Mike sat across the desk as the supervisor offered a scathing assessment of his performance, giving him the lowest rankings Mike had ever received.

After years of dedication and effort, *this* was how he was recognized?! Having his accomplishments ignored and forced to work under the thumb of a villainous manager bent on getting him out of there?

No. The job wasn't "good enough" anymore. This was the final straw. It was time to be done. On the drive home, Mike started thinking about all the things he could do instead. He had his master's degree, so he was educated. He was experienced. He was great with people and had a ton of connections in his industry. Not only was he good at what he did, they had him training others! Just the other day he was teaching a new guy all of his methods and presentation material. Yes, Mike definitely had what it took to do something else. This was definitely the end for him. He would find something new.

You might recognize a little of yourself in Mike. Maybe you've thought about leaving a job even though you're good at it because you just can't take it anymore. Or maybe you're dreaming of something completely different—it might be to finally get in shape, or fall in love, or start a company. It could be to wrestle your finances into submission or to forge a better relationship with your brother. Whatever it is, the key thing is that *you don't have it*. You're not there yet.

In my book *Stories That Stick*, I call this the *gap*: the space between where you are and where you want to be. *Stories That Stick* focused on business gaps; the gap between a product and the customer who didn't understand they needed it. The gap between an important initiative and getting buy-in from the team. The gap between the brand and the way the marketplace sees and understands it. The companies who close the gaps in business best, win.

And the same is true outside of business.

We all have gaps in *life*, too. That space between where we are and where we want to, and on some level believe we can, be. Those gaps are human nature. Without them, we'd have no hopes, no dreams. We wouldn't aspire, strive, or achieve. Without gaps, we wouldn't be *human*.

But while there's nothing more human than dreaming of leaping a gap, there are few things more disheartening than staring at a gap *and never doing anything about it*. Particularly if you've stared at that gap for twenty-five years as Mike had.

Yes. At the time of that disastrous review by that atrocious supervisor, Mike hadn't been working at the company for a few years or even a decade . . . he had been there for *twenty-five years*. And every year, multiple times, he considered leaving.

Maybe you've been in a job like that before (or maybe it was a relationship), a job where, at least every couple of months or so, you wonder, *What am I even doing here?!* There had been plenty of times in the past where Mike was pretty sure the best thing he could do was grab his things (and maybe a few extra pieces of candy off the receptionist's desk), run out, and never, ever look back. But he never did.

In twenty-five years, he never left . . . he always stayed.

And this time was no different.

After the initial shock and frustration wore off during the weekend following his disheartening review, he arrived to work on Monday calm and professional. After all, that's what he was . . . a professional. He kept doing his great work and at his next annual review (yes, another whole year later), he had finally won over his critical supervisor who promoted him to the very top of his, albeit meager, pay scale . . . and so he stayed. Again. However, even more money couldn't quiet the subtle thought that maybe there was something more for him out there.

But whatever that something was, he never took the step to find out. Because somewhere, some unidentifiable force kept him standing on the edge of point A, staring across the void at an undetermined point B, unable to take the first step to journey across the gap.

WHY IS MIKE STUCK?

It's a good question. Mike's smart and motivated—at least when it comes to most things. He has the talent, the connections, and a goal. Yet each time he faces the first step (actually, you know, *quitting*), he falters. And it's not as though he didn't have the opportunity. It kept coming up—different ideas of what he could do if he left this job. He could start his own firm, go into private practice. He had been offered different opportunities by various companies along the way that were specifically tailored to his unique abilities and each time he dreamed about leaving . . . And each time, that little voice starts in his head: *You've got a good job and that's good enough.*

That innocent little statement is what I call a *tip-of-the-iceberg* moment. There is much more to say about that in the chapters ahead, but for now, all you need to know is that, like real icebergs, the part that you see is just a glimpse of something much larger. It's a peek into the underlying stories Mike's been telling himself for longer than he knows. And it's that story that's keeping Mike stuck.

You and I are no different. We also have our tip-of-the-iceberg moments, little glimpses into the larger stories that steer our life.

To rewrite those stories, we need to understand *why* we tell stories in the first place. To do that, we have to go back. Not to a few years ago, or to college, or even to Mike's childhood (or yours). We have to go much further back, back to where the trouble for Mike *really* began.

THE STORYTELLING SPARK

A crazy thing happens about four hundred thousand years ago: *we start to get good at fire.*

This is a far bigger deal than you might think. Fire lets us cook our food, which is about much more than grill marks and searing in the flavor. Cooking food lets us extract more nutrients from our hunting and gathering efforts, and it cuts way down on the amount of chewing we have to do. (Seriously: chimps, who can't do fire, spend some six hours a day just *chewing*.)

All that extra nutrition with less work allows our brains to grow bigger. That helps us get smarter and use our free time to make tools, create language, and eventually invent the iPhone.

But it also does something unexpected: fire makes the day longer. Fire is warm and safe and bright, and that makes it a natural place to gather at a time of day when we tend to be slowing down, biologically getting ready to groove into bedtime.

These two forces—our growing brains and a natural gathering point—lead over time to something even bigger than fire itself: *storytelling*.

Storytelling was a shortcut. It allowed the earlier versions of us to share information about everything from food sources to weather and tools. It enhanced bonding and trust and accelerated learning.[1] And this was especially true around fires. Our ancestors spent most of that time literally having fireside chats. Research into hunter-gathering tribes found that more than 80 percent of firelight conversation was devoted to storytelling.[2] It's no exaggeration to say that storytelling (and a little dose of fire) is what *made* us as a species.

Today, that ancient campfire legacy lives on. Even if you've never taken a single step past the city limits, you've experienced what lighting a few candles can do for the mood. How a little flame can create intimacy and bring out conversation. And haven't we all felt the tug of a screen? That's your ancient campfire biology hijacking your brain. All that sensory stimulation plus the storytelling of social media? It's no wonder you can't look away.

Later research has taken things further. Not only did fire turn us into storytellers, but that newfound ability to spin a tale gave us a host of benefits. Good storytellers, it turns out, are more attractive to potential mates and even have more healthy offspring.[3] Good storytelling can make you a better leader, make you more persuasive, and earn you more money.

THE MOST POWERFUL PERSON IN THE WORLD

There's a story about Steve Jobs from the 1990s, back before Pixar was a household name: he came storming into the break room one day, grabbed a bagel, and asked his team, "Who is the most powerful person in the world?!" The people in the break room, not sure whether it was a hypothetical question but not wanting to evade answering, shouted out a few ideas. Steve said, "No. The storyteller is the most powerful person in the world."

At the time, Jobs was frustrated because Disney was telling better stories than he was.

He told his wide-eyed team, "I am going to be the next great storyteller!" Then he stormed out, bagel in hand. And while this account may be apocryphal, if this really *was* one of Jobs's goals, it appears as though he figured it out. Jobs reinvented multiple industries with his storytelling ability. Innumerable business books and articles have dissected his marketing techniques and his "just one more thing" killer product launches. They're all based on that spark of fire from nearly half a million years ago.

The storytellers, it seems, have inherited the earth.

THE OTHER KIND OF STORY

It's not hard to see why storytelling gave our ancestors such an incredible advantage. The ability to teach, trust, and survive was like jet fuel for our species. And it still is—after hundreds of thousands of years, we're still telling tales and reaping the benefits. The future, still, belongs to the storytellers.

That being said . . .

Somewhere along the way, as our brains developed, we also developed the ability to tell a different kind of story. We developed the neural wiring for what some scientists call an *inner monologue*. Somewhere in our brain, a voice of sorts started to make itself known—almost like a narrator in a movie.

In other words, we weren't just telling stories to each other; we had started telling stories to *ourselves*.

Researchers have many more names for your self-storytelling, like *internal narrative, inner discourse,* or just *self-talk.* You might have your own name for it, like that "little voice" or your "inner critic," or, my personal favorite, "Steven." (Yes, people name their inner voices. Don't judge.)

I simply call this voice your *inner storyteller* because that's what it is. Just like the fires that our early ancestors huddled around, you have an inner campfire of sorts in your mind.

And holding court before the flames is the greatest storyteller in history: *you.*

THE DOUBLE-EDGED STORY SWORD

At its root, a self-story is a habit. It's a pattern of automatic thinking that we're often unaware of. That evolution has automated this storytelling skill in the brain and kept it around for so many millennia is a testament to how useful it must be. Yet, the power of self-story isn't obvious. It makes sense that our ability to tell stories to each other was an advantage. But why would we tell them to *ourselves*?

As you can imagine, it's hard to study an invisible and frequently unconscious story happening inside someone's head. But that hasn't stopped researchers from trying, and their work shows we use self-stories to solve problems, motivate ourselves, make plans, exercise self-control, and to reflect on ourselves.[4]

Look through that list, and you realize that we evolved to use self-stories for the same reasons we evolved to tell stories out loud: *they made us better humans*. Our internal dialogue helped us stay safe, fit into the tribe, and make sense of the world. That, in turn, helped us live longer and have more offspring, which rewarded our odd little habit of talking to ourselves quietly, deep down inside. And the cycle continued. Fast-forward many generations, and you have Mike. And you.

Just as we collect information and share it outwardly in the form of stories with others, we also collect a lifetime of clues about who we are, what we're capable of, what is good and fair, what is responsible, what is the "right" way to live, and we share those stories with a captive audience of one.

Mike had plenty of those stories. The son of a pipe fitter and homemaker, he heard the stories of what it meant to provide for a family. His father worked for Honeywell every single day he was employed. It was a good job, and that was good enough. Mike grew up going to a strict, all-boys Catholic school, and he had his own experiences and memories of what happened when you stepped out of line. As a young man he joined the Navy, then went to college where he met a beautiful woman. They married, and he found a good enough job in his field of study and he worked there as they bought their first home, and as his children were born. He worked there as they built their dream home out in the country. And all along the way, the stories played. *You have a good job. You have security. You have invested five . . . fifteen . . . twenty-five years in this career; it would be irresponsible to throw it away so close to retirement.* Even when a young colleague, whom Mike had trained, left the company and made a small fortune by starting his *own* business doing exactly what Mike had trained him to do with only a fraction of Mike's skill, experience, or charisma . . . even then Mike told himself the story of *the "good job," the secure job*. A story that kept him right where he was.

YOUR INNER SURVIVOR

Like Mike, you have an inner storyteller, and the stories you tell are your own. They are as unique as a fingerprint. Some people experience self-stories as something close to a dialogue in their own voice. Yours may feel like a conversation with someone else.

Your inner storyteller may be something closer to an "inner critic" whispering in your ear, or your self-stories may be more abstract. You may or may not hear a "voice" in your head, narrating your day like a scene from a movie. It doesn't matter—the self-story is there regardless.

Your stories have a job to do, and it's a job that's been carefully honed by evolution. That job is to *protect* you—to keep you alive long enough to continue the species.

But you're not living in a cave, sitting around an open fire trying to explain why that one particular mushroom is a *really* bad idea. You're not living at the brink of survival. Most days, you're trying to bridge a much less dangerous gap—to lose a few pounds, pay your bills, find love, or just deal with a difficult friend or colleague.

But inside your brain, the part of you that is sitting around your inner campfire is still a million years old. And that part of you sees losing your job, or being embarrassed, or failing, or not getting a second date not as disappointments, but as *threats*.

And so your inner storyteller goes to work, weaving a tale that keeps you safe. Like Mike, staying at a job that no longer suits him instead of quitting, your self-stories maintain the status quo and keep you alive for another day—at least as far as your brain is concerned.

MIKE AND THE STORY THAT GOT HIM NOWHERE

There is something I haven't told you about Mike.

He's my dad.

In June of 2009, I was driving to a morning spin class when my father called. I knew it must be something serious; he didn't usually call, and never in the morning. In his voice, I could hear he was defeated, stressed, lost, exhausted, and, most difficult to hear, *ashamed*.

"They let me go," he said. After thirty-six years, and with no consideration of his tenure, the company cut the funding for the entire program my father had created. He was one of their most senior people. He had achieved one of the highest levels in the organization. He had dedicated his entire adult life to their cause, endured decades of struggle and frustration and bureaucratic office nonsense, and now they were letting him go with a measly severance and a fraction of the retirement he was a mere three years from achieving.

It was heartbreaking. For all of us.

However, looking back, even more heartbreaking than the fact that he lost his job was what kept him there in the first place. Though he had all the talent, all the connections, all the skills and experience he needed to break out on his own, his stories didn't let him leave. Any time he came close, his inner storyteller would start chanting: "It's irresponsible to leave a perfectly good job," and "Long-term employment equals security, and security is better than risk," and "Don't throw away ten-plus, then twenty-plus, then thirty-plus years of experience—it's better to stay." These stories were there to keep him safe yet, in the end, left him out in the cold.

In the end, stories that are meant to keep us from harm often keep us from possibility, too.

THE PROBLEM WITH YOUR STORY

I'm happy to report that Mike has made the best of a bad situation. Today, my father plays in two bands: an acoustic guitar duo with his friend Randy (they used to play together in college) and a rock band with my mom and a couple of their friends from the condo complex where they live. My dad also started investing in real estate and owns several condos in their complex and has become quite the vacation rental mogul at the age of sixty-five, proof that it's never too late to start a new story . . . (but we will get to that later).

That being said, Mike's story is not unique. Millions of others settle for a muted version of life: they use mustard-yellow stories to build their yellow brick roads and end up at an olive-green city instead of an emerald one. Some get their wakeup call from the poppy field early on; some get it days before retirement. Some get it while isolated and unexpectedly teaching homeschool.

Regardless of when or how it comes, the source of the problem is the same: *your inner storyteller isn't well aligned with the outer world.*

The outer world has changed. It's not as dangerous as your inner storyteller perceives it to be. You don't *need* to be saved quite so frequently from near-extinction.

Yet, those stories still have you in their grip. *That's* the problem. The problem isn't that you're a storyteller by nature; that is still one of your greatest strengths. And it's also not a problem that you tell stories to yourself.

Where things become problematic is when those stories are creating your reality—*and it's not the reality you want.*

LIFE IMITATES STORY

How Stories Create Your Reality

Beware the stories you read or tell;
subtly, at night, beneath the waters of consciousness,
they are altering your world.

—BEN OKRI

Meet Roberta.

Roberta is a landscape architect. By all accounts, she's good at it. If you need to create a beautiful outdoor space—a park, a cemetery, a residential community—Roberta would be your go-to.

Like great landscape architecture itself, it's hard to tell how old Roberta is. She's impeccably put together. Long, silver, stylish hair. Trim. Well spoken. She might be fifty-five. She might be eighty-five. Roberta has this beautiful, timeless quality.

Looking at her, you'd never know she'd recently beaten stage three cancer.

Or that her marriage had dissolved.

Or that she'd recently moved.

Or that she'd been laid off.

That's a long list of obstacles for anyone. But there's more. Roberta's now in the process of reinventing herself as a health coach. A full-on career change at the age of—well, I'm not sure (that whole timeless thing). All I know is that Roberta has come to me with a problem.

The issue, Roberta tells me, is that she isn't an entrepreneur. She's a designer. Roberta doesn't know how to sell things.

And, as a result, she's *not* selling things. Including herself, which is a problem. Because after the cancer and the breakup and the layoff, this is now how Roberta is supposed to make money. And she's not making any.

Roberta is standing on Cliff A, staring across what feels like an uncrossable distance, at Cliff B. The gap feels impossible, so much so that she's considering throwing in the towel on pursuing her Emerald City dreams and just getting whatever entry-level job she can find.

The crazy thing is that *the gap isn't actually that big*. Roberta has everything she needs to succeed in her new work. Looking at her, talking to her, I can tell she's perfectly suited for it. The more Roberta talks, the more I want her to be *my* health coach. She's amazing.

But I'm the only person Roberta's talking to. She's not out there telling anyone else about what she can offer. And the reason is, you guessed it, *her stories*.

Evolution, we now know, has turned Roberta into a master storyteller. Not just of the campfire story, but of a different kind—an internal *self-story*. The question now is not whether that story is *there*. If you've read this far, you know there's a whole storytelling world at work within you. The question now is, *why does that story matter?* Right now, in your life today. *Why* and *how* do these inner stories have so much power, and *what* does that power mean?

It's one thing to believe that a self-story might have kept us safe from danger in a world where risks were higher. Or that it may have bonded us more closely with our tribe to help us prosper. But how does a self-story keep us from crossing the modern gaps we face, like getting that promotion, finding a romantic partner, or paying the bills?

Fortunately, a growing body of research has uncovered why stories do the weird and wonderful things they do—including predicting your future. And while there is still a lot of understanding and uncovering to be done, it seems the power of a story starts less with *once upon a time*, and more with *once upon a brain*.

STORIES TAKE YOUR BRAIN HOSTAGE

As I mentioned earlier, I opened my last book with a story about my husband being mentally kidnapped by a story. It told the unlikely (especially if you know my husband) tale of how a remarkable marketing story had convinced Michael that we should start a cologne empire.

We did not start said empire. And it was probably never a good idea. But at the time, in the grips of the story the salesclerk told us, it was The. Most. Amazing. Idea. Ever.

Michael is no sucker. He's a brilliant, thoughtful guy. But he also has the same neurological legacy that you, Roberta, and I have. We are *all* descended from storytellers, and that has literally shaped our biology. Thanks to evolution, before stories change our lives, they first change our *brains*.

Here's a much-simplified version of what happens in your brain and body when you hear a great story:

1. *Storytelling captures your attention*. Hearing a story triggers the release of *cortisol*, the hormone that grabs your awareness. What began as a tool to keep us focused on that rustle in the jungle or stealthy footstep in the night has been co-opted by story to keep you attentive.[1]
2. *Storytelling helps you learn*. Once the story-triggered cortisol has grabbed your attention, *dopamine* steps in. A part of your reward and learning system, dopamine gives the story the emotional

charge it needs to keep you engaged to reach the finish and to help you remember the details for later.[2]

3. *Storytelling helps you trust.* Finally, *oxytocin*, the "trust" or "love" molecule, arrives on the scene. It makes you empathetic, helping you identify with the characters in a story and deepening your emotional connection to the outcome.[3]

The result is something akin to a mental kidnapping, where stories grab your nervous system and hold it hostage.

If you've ever been spellbound by a film or been so immersed in a book that time seemed to vanish, you've experienced that power. If you've ever cried out "No!" at a cliffhanger in your favorite series that left you waiting for the next episode, you know what I mean. Try as you might, it's unavoidable: a great story grabs your brain and doesn't let go.

YOUR BRAIN THINKS STORIES ARE REAL

It's one thing that a story has the ability to overthrow the brain, to fully infiltrate it and, in its siege, like a puppet master holding the strings, impact your thoughts, emotions, and behavior. But the other incredible relationship between the brain and a story is how the brain reacts to it—how it can turn thought into reality, fiction into fact, and future into now.

Imagination vs. Reality

I grew up in rural Minnesota in a home on a hill surrounded by tall grass. To any Midwesterner, the words "tall grass" are immediately followed by thoughts of a particularly detestable insect, the tick. Reddish-brownish. Eight legs. Two pinchers for a mouth and, if you look closely, white markings on its back. (Fun fact: Male wood ticks have two lines down their back like suspenders, and females have a half-circle around their neck like a string of pearls. Be gross, but make it fashion.) I remember tick checks as a kid, and now, when I take my kids back to Minnesota in the summer or out to Montauk where there are even *more* ticks, I am the one conducting them. All it takes is the sight of one tick on my kid, and suddenly, it feels like they are crawling all over me. You know the feeling—even reading this, is your skin crawling a bit?

It turns out this weird connection between your imagination and your body isn't that, well, weird. Your brain, it seems, isn't particularly good at distinguishing imagination from reality. For example, if I ask you to read words that describe odors—like *oregano* or *cinnamon*—the part of your brain most associated with smell will light up. If I ask you to read words like *scissors* or *glasses,* that same region stays dark.[4] The same is true of words about body actions[5] or textures[6]—they light up the relevant regions of your brain that would be active if you were actually *doing* or *touching*. To your brain, the words are similar to the real thing.

You can easily experience this reality-imagination connection by picturing a lemon in detail—your mouth will almost certainly water. For some people, just *imagining* staring over the edge of a steep cliff is enough to make their heart race and their feet tingle as the areas of the brain associated with fear are activated. I have a hard time in theaters and stadiums—the steep, slanted staircases make me feel like my body is going to involuntarily throw myself down, taking out every peanut and popcorn salesman who happens to be in my way.

This imagination-reality connection (or, more accurately, *confusion*) is an advantage in business. It's why storytelling is so powerful in sales, particularly if you're selling something the person can't see, feel, touch, hold, or experience. If you're selling insurance, you can't hand the potential client a bottle of it and ask them to take a whiff to see how much safer they feel. Selling the invisible is tough, and those who are best at it are those who use stories to tap into this imagination-reality connection. Through story, they can make a potential customer *feel* the emotions associated with the product or service.

However, while storytelling is great in business where stories are consciously constructed, the blurred lines between reality and imagination can backfire when it comes to our unconscious self-storytelling. Reliving the embarrassing story of trying (and failing) to do a pull-up in front of your first-grade class every time you walk into a gym as an adult could very well keep you from getting in shape. Experiencing the story of the infidelity of an ex-partner every time your new flame doesn't pick up the phone could keep you from a healthy relationship.

Truth vs. Fiction

My daughter was working on an essay for a third-grade writing assignment in which her job was to recall a moment in her life and tell the story. As you might imagine, my kids have a lot of practice when it comes to telling stories, and a few days later, my daughter proclaimed that the teachers loved her essay. They praised the emotion and the detail and the way she painted a picture of the scary situation with her words.

"What did you write about?" I asked her.

"That time I got knocked down and run over by those two big dogs on the golf course," she said.

She then proceeded to tell me the whole story. How one evening we were walking on the cart path on the golf course where we used to live, and how there were friends and neighbors out playing with their dogs, and how someone threw the green tennis ball with the ball-throwing device, and how both big dogs ran after it, and then both big dogs ran back and how they ran right into her and knocked her down. "Remember, Mama? You were so scared."

Yes, I did remember. It was exactly as she described it—except for one part.

"Sweet girl," I said slowly. "*You* didn't get knocked down by the dogs. Your brother did."

She insisted it was her.

It wasn't. It was her brother.

The look on her face when she realized a whole experience, a whole story, in her life wasn't actually hers is a look I wish you could see right now; it's the same look you might have when you start looking into some of your own stories. Because whether or not the story is true, whether or not it actually happened to *you*, your brain loves a story. And if it's close enough, even if it doesn't confuse the characters the way my daughter did, your brain will absorb it and adopt it and replay it as its own.

This integration of a story into the fiber of your being as if it were your own doesn't just happen to eight-year-old girls writing essays. I had a dear friend who lost her cousin in a tragic car accident. The husband, his pregnant wife, and their toddler were traveling over the holidays in Minnesota. They hit a patch of black ice, and their car went hurtling out of control and into oncoming traffic. They were struck by an eighteen-wheeler. The wife and daughter survived, the husband and unborn baby did not. I was home from graduate school, visiting my family in Minnesota the night it happened. I was actually getting ready to meet that very friend for dinner when she called to cancel last minute and told me the news. There was something about that story that stuck with me. I knew at that moment that I would never move back to Minnesota. Driving in the winter is a terrifying endeavor—I'd been in multiple weather-related incidents and lost several classmates to winter car accidents.

Don't get me wrong—there are many reasons to love and live in Minnesota. Michael and I have even talked about moving there for the kids' high school years, but every time I think of it, I am taken back to that story. I am sitting in the passenger seat when the car careens out of control. I feel my heart rate tick up, and I can see the chaos unfold around me. It's like it's my story. And even though it isn't, I decide each time to never live in Minnesota again.

Not only can our brains not tell truth from reality, but we also can't always tell *our* truths from someone else's.

Telling vs. Doing

Perhaps the most fascinating aspect of this brain/story connection is that storytelling not only lights up your brain but can also *change* it. Visualization has been shown to change the brains of athletes and musicians, demonstrating that the "mental practice" of a skill can make changes in the same area of your brain that would develop if you did the skill in real life.

In 2016, Michael Phelps became the most decorated Olympic athlete of all time, finishing the 2016 games in Rio de Janeiro with a lifetime total of twenty-eight medals.

Phelps is a phenom. He has the genetic physical gifts of an athlete built to swim, the competitive nature of a winner. But he's also spent years honing his visualization skills. His coach Bob Bowman taught Phelps how to vividly rehearse races in his mind *hundreds of times* so that on race day, he's on autopilot. Phelps visualizes not just every step of a successful race but also the possibilities of something going wrong—a slip at the start, a ripped suit, or even leaky goggles.

As his coach said, "He may be the best ever in terms of visualization . . . when he swims the race, he's already programmed his nervous system."[7]

At the Beijing Olympics, Phelps *did* have a problem with his goggles. In the 200m butterfly event, his goggles began leaking as soon as he hit the water. The problem got worse the longer he swam. By the end of the race, Phelps couldn't see the finish wall and was swimming mostly blind.

It was the exact problem he'd imagined. And it didn't matter— Michael was prepared for the obstacle and had practiced the swim mentally so many times that he didn't *need* to see. He swam the race just as he'd envisioned, won the gold, and broke the world record.

The lesson in all of this? It doesn't matter if the story happened in the past, happened to you, or hasn't even happened at *all*. You are telling stories to yourself, and they are changing you.

YOUR STORIES WILL LEAD YOU TOWARD — OR AWAY FROM — YOUR DESTINATION

So, your brain loves stories. And at a neurological level, it can't effectively tell the difference between fiction and nonfiction, between imagination and reality, and between present and future. In each case, a story can make *real things happen in your brain and body.*

But here's the final piece in the puzzle. Not only are our minds entranced by the call of the seductive story-sirens, but stories *change the way we behave* as well.

In 1964, a Harvard psychologist named Robert Rosenthal arrived at an elementary school in San Francisco with a brand-new IQ test. Rosenthal had received the principal's blessing to administer this new IQ test—Rosenthal's Harvard Test of Inflected Acquisition—to the students at Spruce Elementary.[8]

The results were exciting. In each classroom, the test uncovered small groups of children who had "unusual potential" to grow intellectually. Rosenthal compiled lists of these talented prospects and passed them on to the teachers.

Later, Rosenthal returned to retest the student IQs. Sure enough, the students who'd been identified as being extra intelligent had made much greater gains in their test scores.

At this point, it's not surprising that smart kids got smarter. There's no story there. The twist is that the smart kids never *were* smarter. Rosenthal's fancy test was just a run-of-the-mill IQ test. And the kids with all that intellectual potential? They were just chosen at random. It wasn't the high-potential kids who improved; it was the ones who were *labeled* with higher potential.

The kids had no idea there was a fake story at work—it was the teachers at Spruce Elementary who were seduced. With new expectations firmly in place, the teachers launched into their school year and then immediately demonstrated another glitch/feature in the human brain: *confirmation bias*.

Confirmation bias refers to our tendency to favor information that backs up what we already believe. Believing a student was gifted, the teachers began to notice, recall, and interpret student behavior in a way that met that belief. Eventually, their belief in the test results became a self-fulfilling prophecy. They treated the kids differently. The kids felt different. Everyone had a new story. The story about the smarter cohort of kids went from pure fiction to fact.

Rosenthal and his partner, Lenore Jacobson, named his finding the Pygmalion effect, after the Greek myth of the sculptor who falls in love with his own statue, which the gods eventually bring to life. The effect describes the self-fulfilling prophecy wherein high expectations lead to better results. It's the science behind the oft-quoted saying attributed to Henry Ford: "Whether you think you can or you think you can't, you're right."

Rosenthal's experiment showed that *what we believe matters*. Since Rosenthal's first experiment, the effect has been reproduced elsewhere, from courtroom trials[9] and athletic performance[10] to nursing home outcomes[11] and sales performance.[12] In each case, we rise to our expectations.

In other words, *we literally become our stories*.

SAD STORIES AND TRAGIC TALES

This poses a problem.

If we're such natural storytellers, and stories create our reality, and ultimately, we *become* them, you would think we'd have evolved into naturally positive storytellers. Unfortunately, that's not how evolution rolled things out. Instead, we love ourselves a big, bad story.

One frigid November evening in 2020, I was standing on the city sidewalk with a network camera crew waiting to film my part of a national news clip that would include my thoughts on the closing of New York City public schools during the coronavirus pandemic. We picked the spot, they got the lighting set, mic'd me up, and then the crew and I made small talk until it was showtime.

We had our pick of newsworthy things to talk about, but at some point, it occurred to me that we were focused on the bad ones. Why were we regurgitating the pandemic challenges and not talking about the increasing good vaccine news? Why the economic problems and not the seasonal spike in retail sales?

That focus became the focus of our conversation. "Why," I wondered aloud, "do we always talk about the bad stories? Even in casual conversation? I mean, this is the first time we've met. Why don't I tell you about the great thing that happened to a friend of mine this morning or the breakthrough I had at work?"

The crew member sighed. "You know, we talk about this every morning in our newsroom meeting—what stories are we going to share today? And while there are exciting things happening, ultimately the scary stories are what people want to hear."

There was conflict in his voice. As if a part of him believed that people needed more hope, not fear. But the news is business. And the bad stories, the scary stories—they pay the bills. They are what people tune in for. Like moths to the bad-news flame, the scary headline is the one we click on. Move over sex; you may sell, but fear sells more.

While your stories won't necessarily make the news, this obsession with the negative lives within each of us. If you have ever posted something on social media—perhaps something even just a little vulnerable—99 percent of the comments were almost certainly positive, cheering you on, validating and celebrating you. And then there was *one*. That *one* person who said something mean or put you down. Which of those comments can you recite word for word? My guess is only one of them—the bad one.

I once posted an emotional, endearing story on Instagram. I don't remember what the story was exactly, but I *do* remember a lot of people offered words of support and gratitude. And then there was one woman who said: "How dare you not post about Christopher Columbus on Columbus Day. How dare you erase him from the pages of history." Admittedly, it stands out because it truly was a new level of crazy, but *why on earth* do I remember that comment and not any of the others?

It turns out that being just a little negative helped us survive. The more tuned in to danger and risk your ancestors were, the more likely they were to live longer. Assuming a noise in the brush was a bear, not a cool breeze, was a survival advantage.

The result is that we have what scientists call a *negativity bias*. Research shows we tend to remember traumatic incidents better and that we think more frequently about negative things. We also learn more from negative experiences and tend to make decisions based more on negative information than positive.[13] This tendency influences our stories, too, giving them a negative slant.

There are two takeaways here. The first is that you don't have to feel bad for your collection of negative stories and your tendency to beat yourself up or fear the worst. Not only is it normal, but your negative bias is what helped your long line of ancestors survive long enough to produce you. If the early cave-person versions of you had been diehard optimists, you wouldn't be here!

The second takeaway is *awareness*. It's important to be aware that while your stories are creating your life, those stories tend to be fearful. Cautious. Overly critical. As a result, your unconscious storyteller is leading you to stay safe in a world where physical safety isn't your primary concern. Which explains why the bricks we've been laying, the stories we've been telling ourselves, aren't leading us any closer to the Emerald City. They're just leading us in circles, keeping us feeling safe, but stuck in places that, though they may not be excellent, at least they are familiar.

Rosenthal, the Pygmalion effect guy, was aware of this. In his experiment, he singled out random students as intellectual "growth spurters." He could have done the opposite, randomly identifying the intellectual "losers," but fortunately, he knew better. Even before testing his theory on kids, Rosenthal had done more or less the same thing with rats, showing how the expectations of scientists could lead their rats to perform differently. He knew that, applied to kids, a negative label would be unethical and harmful.

But the opposite of the Pygmalion effect exists, nonetheless. It's called the *golem effect*, and it describes how low expectations lead to poorer results. When we let our negative stories take the lead, we're allowing the golem effect to step into our lives. Rosenthal would not be impressed.

I want you to remember this as we move into part II of the book. Your negativity bias is going to show itself as you start turning your attention to your own stories. Know that, at first, you're going to find it easier to recall your negative stories—they're going to be top of mind—and that you might struggle to come up with stories that illustrate another, more positive, side of you. When you do, remember the negativity bias. It tells us that there really is another side to your experiences—you just need to practice a little to bring it to life. Your inner storyteller can be turned to the light. You just need a little time and the right tools.

ROBERTA GETS HER GROOVE BACK

What does all this mean for Roberta, our landscape architect turned health coach?

Roberta could tell she was resisting doing the things she needed to do to grow her new business. She'd taken the training. She was confident in her skills. But like any business, she needed *clients*. And she wasn't doing the work to get them.

"I'm doing things," she tells me. "But I'm not doing what I should do."

Roberta knows she's facing the gap. She can feel it. But she can't quite put her finger on the hidden *why*.

As we talk, however, I can hear Roberta's hidden story start to emerge, revealing itself in tiny phrases. Little tip-of-the-iceberg statements like *I'm not an entrepreneur.* At one point, in reference to the selling she knows she needs to do, she comes right out and tells me, "I'm not a rainmaker."

Roberta's story, one backed by a lifetime of experience that she's pointing to over and over, is that she's not the kind of person that runs a business. She's creative, a designer. She doesn't sell. She doesn't self-promote. That's someone else's job.

But that's a self-fulfilling story. Every time Roberta tells a compelling, vivid story from her past about just how *not* a salesperson she is, the story stops her from taking action. She doesn't make the phone call. She doesn't work on her social branding. She doesn't do any of the hundreds of tiny actions—all of which she is *fully capable of*—that add up to new clients and a successful small business. When Roberta says it's someone else's job, then it *is* someone else's job. But in her company of one, that means it's *no one's* job.

Roberta *is* the golem effect. She's literally not doing what she needs to do to cross the gap *because of a story she's telling herself.* And so she's stuck. Her story is creating her reality. She is reaching the level of her limited expectations. Her current high-water mark is set by her negative self-stories.

But ultimately, our stories belong to *us*, not the other way around. Over the course of a few weeks, Roberta learns to shift that story and replace it with a new one. She finds evidence from her past that she *does* have what it takes to be an entrepreneur. In fact, she realizes she really is—and has been—a salesperson all along.

By the time I speak to Roberta for the third time, it's like I'm speaking to a different person. Same Roberta, yet different. She's timeless and elegant as always. But now she's *energized*. Armed with her new stories, she's taking action on the things she always knew she should be doing. And it's paying off. She's booked two new clients. She's making money. She's rewriting her story.

A NEW STORY TO CLOSE THE GAP

Like Roberta, we're all facing the A to B gap. And in between that gap are *stories*—the stories that *create* that gap, and, as we'll discover, the stories that can *bridge* it. Although the particulars of her gap may look different from yours or mine, the struggle is the same: what to do about the space between where you are and where you'd like to be.

Determining what to do is complicated by what seems like a perfect storm:

- We're highly influenced by stories—they're wired right into us.
- Furthermore, our brains can't always tell reality from imagination, truth from fiction, or present from future.
- Finally, that story, true or false, *changes* what we believe we're capable of, and in turn, *how we behave.*

Or, as the *New York Times* so succinctly put it, stories "stimulate the brain and even change how we act in life."[14]

When you cross a powerful story with reality, *reality changes*. The story, true or false, changes your future, for better or worse. Tell your brain a story, and it will find what it needs to make it true.

That's a challenging gap to bridge.

Or is it?

We can see now that your life isn't a story about the things that have happened to you; the things that have happened to you *become* a story that you tell back to yourself and cause you to feel, think, act, and *live* a certain way. The stories you tell yourself are the ultimate self-fulfilling prophecy.

The life you have right now is the result of many, many stories. Some small, some large. Some powerful, some nearly insignificant. Combined, they've helped to create the reality you live in—the friends you have, the money you earn, the decisions you make.

So if the stories you have been telling yourself have gotten you to where you are now, but you actually want to be somewhere else . . . what happens if you change them? What happens if you choose different ones?

CHOOSE YOUR STORY, CHANGE YOUR LIFE

How Rewriting Your Stories Can Transform Your Future

> The story we tell ourselves could very well be centered on the
> things that have happened in our past that we cannot change—
> but we cannot change them. What we can change, if we choose,
> is the story we tell ourselves.
>
> — SETH GODIN

It was a beautiful Thursday afternoon in October. I was sitting at my favorite lunch spot in the city, eating and editing an upcoming article, when my phone rang. It was my agent calling to see if I would be able to speak for one of her clients.

I was just about to take another bite when she said the name of the company.

I dropped my fork and almost fell out of my chair.

You know how people tell you to make a list of your dream clients? The ones you would just *die* to work with for whatever reason? Or maybe you and your partner have one of those lists of celebrities you're allowed to make out with if you ever get the chance? Potential issues with Michael aside, an invitation to speak for this client was like Bradley Cooper or Zac Efron asking if I was available to be their date to the Met Gala.

The difference, however, was that this event was not going to be as easy as a stroll down the red carpet. This event was intense. A *really* big deal. It would be a roomful of the company's top leaders—smart, skilled, successful individuals who do not mess around. They know excellence when they see it, so there's no phoning it in, no faking it. Not only that, but I knew in my soul that if I did well here, there could be a possibility for something else in the future. Which also meant that if I bombed, it was all over.

Fortunately, I was 100 percent ready. I knew this audience. I'd been following them. Studying them. I'd been presenting for other companies in their space. I was already beyond prepared, and I knew it. *This* was the moment I'd been waiting for, and holy moly, it was finally here!

I immediately started imagining myself standing on their stage the following spring, sharing my story and living my dream—

Then my agent said: "It's actually kind of an emergency. The speaker they originally hired is no longer able to present. They need you on Saturday. You'll need to be on a plane tomorrow."

And my heart stopped.

Tomorrow? I couldn't do *tomorrow*. Typically, events book six to twelve months in advance. I couldn't begin to wrap my head around tomorrow.

Yet here it was. My dream client. What might be one of the biggest moments in my career. The easiest *yes* ever.

Instead, I asked, "Can I give you a call back in a bit?"

There was a pause. My agent also knew how incredible this opportunity was and was stunned I didn't immediately agree.

"You've got one hour," she said. We hung up the phone.

I was at a self-storytelling crossroads. It was as if the overgrowth had suddenly cleared, and the yellow brick road was revealed in all its glory right before my eyes, the Emerald City almost within view. The obvious answer was—well, obvious: scream *Yes!*, pack my bag, and head to Vegas on the next flight out.

Instead, with that single opportunity, a set of automatic self-stories were triggered—stories I didn't even know were *there*.

Can you guess what stories were holding me back? From what I've told you so far, you might think it was a spiral of professional self-doubt. Sure, I was "prepared," but prepared enough for the biggest client of my career thus far on a moment's notice? No way. Maybe I was telling myself stories of how much time I need to be "fully ready," for such a huge opportunity or another time when I "wasn't ready," and I flopped. Those would be the obvious guesses for stories that were holding me back.

Yes. They're good guesses. But they're wrong. I was ready, and I knew it.

The self-stories in play were even worse, even more debilitating.

The entire time I considered the career-changing opportunity, all I could think was, *I'm a terrible mother.*

I was already supposed to leave on Sunday for an event on Monday, another on Tuesday, and yet another on Wednesday. Six months from now I could do, but tomorrow?! *What kind of mother leaves her children for so long? So often?*

Then my storytelling machinery really took off. I told myself the stories of all the field trips I'd missed. Of the pickups and drop-offs I was never there for. Of the number of times my kids went to someone else's house because I wasn't in town to host the playdate. And the comparisons! I told myself the stories of how my mom was always home when I was in elementary school. How she'd left her career to be home for us.

And here I was contemplating a spontaneous trip to Vegas?

I walked the two blocks home from the restaurant in a daze. By the time I came through the door and told Michael I had some news, he thought someone was dead. And when I told him who wanted to hire me, he was visibly confused.

"But you love them," he said.

I nodded.

"You've always wanted to speak for them," he said.

I nodded.

"But . . . you're . . ." his mouth fell open a little . . . "*sad* about it?"

I hung my head and nodded.

(Men. Sometimes I really feel for them.)

I told him I had now less than an hour to make my decision. I went into the bathroom, knelt on the floor, and cried.

An hour later, I had made my choice.

And I wasn't wrong. It was one of the biggest decisions of my life.

IF IT'S SO EASY, WHY IS IT SO HARD?

When I tell this story to my friends and colleagues who are familiar with the keynote speaking business and this company in particular, the fact that I didn't shout *YES!* before the agent even finished the question is baffling. And while we could spend our whole lives playing Monday morning quarterback, trying to analyze our choices at each of these various crossroads, there is an underlying pattern for all of them.

Based on what we know now, it's time to take a closer look at the difference between the way we *think* the world works and how it *really* works. As you might have guessed, the two are not the same, and how we see events in our lives and make decisions is a little trickier than meets the untrained eye.

We have been taught that the way we operate in the world is *clear*—that our thoughts and actions are conscious and rational. We think that things happen, we respond to those things, and that's how we get our results. It's a tidy package that looks like this:

A thing happens. You respond to that thing. There is a result.

WHAT WE THINK HAPPENS

EVENT → RESPONSE → RESULT

Pretty straightforward, right? This sequence of events happens all day, every day, in a hundred different ways across all areas of our life, and the linear nature makes it all appear so simple.

The "events" can be anything: Sometimes the event involves other people and could be a conversation or an interaction. Sometimes the event is a digital one—an email, a comment, a text. Sometimes the event is an actual event, like a birthday party or a doctor's appointment. The event could be checking your bank account. It could be an alert on your phone or that moment when the server brings you the dessert menu and asks if you've left any room (as if dessert is ever about physical space in the digestive system).

Anything you can have a response to counts as an event, and the result is what follows. That result can be immediate, yes, but it can also compound slowly over time and leave you shaking your head and asking yourself, "How did I even *get* here?"

Let's take a look at a few examples:

1. Your alarm goes off early in the morning. (Event.)
2. You hit snooze for the next hour. (Response.)
3. You sleep through your workout, and so don't exercise that day. (Result.)

1. Someone reaches out, out of the blue, with a huge opportunity for you. (Event.)
2. You start sketching out ideas but never get around to submitting an idea. (Response.)
3. You miss the opportunity. (Result.)

1. You find shoes/face cream/a car you really want but can't afford. (Event.)
2. You buy it anyway. (Response.)
3. You go further into debt. (Result.)

1. You meet someone new, have a great conversation, would like to see them again. (Event.)
2. You don't ask for a way to connect beyond that interaction. (Response.)
3. You never see them again. (Result.)

Whether you have found yourself in one of these situations personally, or they sound like examples from the lives of your friends and family, don't you find yourself wanting to yell at the page? *Duh! Obviously, if you are trying to improve your health, don't hit snooze. If you're trying to advance your career, send the proposal back ASAP. If you desire to have more money, don't finance expensive things. If you're looking to find a partner, don't let a great one get away without at least making an effort.*

Yet, that's exactly what happens. We don't do the obvious thing, the thing that, in hindsight, is so painfully clear, so simple.

Clearly, there is something going on here. If the path from point A to B is a straight line from event to response to result, then why aren't we all dancing and *tra-lah-lah*-ing around our emerald cities right now?

There must be more to it. And there is.

THE LITTLE BLACK BOX

Let's take a moment here to review what we already know.

1. As humans, we are wired for stories. We crave them. We want to hear them. We find meaning in telling and sharing them. Stories are as much a part of us as the air that moves through our lungs and the blood that flows through our veins.
2. Not only do we share and take in stories with and from others, but there is also an entire storytelling world *inside* you that is taking your brain hostage and creating a reality of its own that either leads you toward or away from your desired destination.

What you likely suspect is that while on the surface it seems pretty easy to retrace the steps that got us those results, something *else* is happening. Something else happens between the event and the response that leads to undesirable results.

The truth is, there is an invisible step in the process that we're barely aware of.

The *story* step.

Rather than directly and consciously responding to the world around us, we're using stories to *interpret* and *inform* what happens to us, and those stories are changing how we *respond* and *behave*, which in turn directly impacts our results. Like this:

WHAT REALLY HAPPENS

$$\boxed{\text{EVENT}} \rightarrow \boxed{\text{STORY}} \rightarrow \boxed{\text{RESPONSE}} \rightarrow \boxed{\text{RESULT}}$$

Between the event and the response, something happens within us. Something so quick that, like a magician dropping a black cloth and turning a dove into a bunny, it's almost undetectable. Every event that happens in our life goes into an internal storytelling "black box" for processing. In that box, our stories mix with reality, and it is only *after* their combustion that we act.

That black box—the hidden world of storytelling inside us—holds the secret to closing the gap between you and anything you desire. If you've ever felt there is an invisible barrier to achieving whatever it is you seek, that's because there is! And you need look no further than getting control over the stories you are telling yourself.

And while I'll never tell you that gaining control of those stories is easy (we'll talk more about what is working against you in a minute), and while some may have more negative stories to wrangle than others as a result of systemic inequities, some pretty incredible changes are possible if you do.

THE DIFFERENCE TAKING CONTROL OF A STORY MAKES

In the final few weeks of 2020, I introduced a group of twenty-eight individuals to the power of self-storytelling. Each of them noted an area of their life where they felt old stories might be holding them back. Through a series of group sessions and four thirty-minute one-on-one sessions, I walked them through the process I am about to teach you. Much as we've done thus far in this book, we first discussed the power our stories have over us and why. Then, we worked through each step in the self-storytelling process I will share in part II to identify the stories that were holding them back and gain control over them by replacing those stories with better stories, *chosen* stories.

Before the first session, the participants filled out a survey that asked a series of questions designed to determine their overall satisfaction with life as well as a few more related categories such as fear of failure, optimism, and anxiety.

Twenty-six of the participants completed the entire program and, after at least two weeks of implementing this approach, were then sent the survey a second time. The results, which due to the small sample size are only directional in nature, were encouraging.

Overall, participants experience a higher satisfaction with life, with more than half of those that were previously dissatisfied reporting their lives were now close to ideal and describing the conditions of their life as excellent. Additionally, their level of optimism increased, while participants also reported a reduced fear of failure. Before the program, 88 percent of participants felt that they were afraid of failing in somewhat difficult situations when a lot depends on them. This number decreased by more than 40 percent. Subsequently, the number of people being afraid of tasks they are unable to solve decreased by more than 50 percent whereas the feeling of anxiety decreased by 39 percent. Additionally, before starting the program, 19 percent of people felt that it was pointless to keep working on something that was too difficult for them. After the program, this percent dropped to zero.

As impressive as the numbers were, their sentiments during the final sessions had even more of an impact:

- "I feel lighter, less worry. *You are enough. You are more than enough.* Those are the things that started coming into my thoughts and mind; . . . that was powerful to me. A very different mindset."
- "[My husband said], 'You have changed over the past couple of weeks.' And I thought about it and realized my mindset . . . It's just completely different. I feel more positive now because I'm saying nice things to myself."
- "I started out and I was like, *I don't know how helpful this is going to be. . .* But I feel like my emotions don't control my behaviors as much. It made it easier to make good decisions."
- "I don't view myself as a failure anymore because I've been able to uncover the stories that I was telling myself and realized that it was completely false, that it was something that I created in my head."
- "I feel very much more open and free. And I have more confidence, too—to take an opportunity that previously I might've said, well, that's not for me. I'm not good enough. Why bother?"
- "Seeing all of that and putting it all together, it's like I can dream again; I can see the future."
- "It definitely worked. Everything that I've been able to tell and write and do, it has had a lasting impression. It's been a complete transformation for me. This is going to change everything, and I'm so grateful for that."
- "I've built a lot of resilience. I would always default to the road of complacency and status quo . . . [Now] it's like, *Well, that's not true; I can turn that around.*"

This is not the last time you will hear about these participants. In fact, many of their stories and subsequent transformations are included in the following chapters as proof or, at the very least, inspiration and example of what is possible when you follow the self-storytelling process.

"ALL YA GOTTA DO IS . . ."

We have a running joke in our house. Anytime Michael or I lay out a plan that is *way* simpler said than done, and we catch ourselves doing it, we follow up the plan by saying in a goofy voice, "All ya gotta do is . . ."

"All ya gotta do is write five thousand words a day for two weeks, and you'll have a book," when writing five thousand words *period* can be mentally excruciating.

"All ya gotta do is get the stomach flu for three days, and you'll lose ten pounds," when the stomach flu is the worst.

"All ya gotta do is grow your Instagram following to one million," when that is a *long* process.

The phrase comes from many years ago when I was gifted a set of DVDs (I told you it was many years ago). Michael and I watched them together one night while I folded the laundry. The DVDs were filmed at a live event where a guru was teaching his students how to make millions the same way he did.

"The formula is simple," he would say in a tone that was equally encouraging and condescending. "All ya gotta do is sell a monthly subscription priced at $49 a month to 500 people, sell 100 digital courses at $500 apiece to 250 people, and host four events a year at a ticket price of $2,000 to 100 people and you'll be making over a million dollars a year."

Sounds simple, right? And I suppose in a way it is. It's pretty much just multiplication. But *easy?* Ha! Ask anyone who's tried. Even if they achieved it, if they told you it's easy, *they're lying*.

The same is true for taking control of the stories you tell yourself.

"All ya gotta do is tell yourself a better story."

Sounds easy. But in reality, it's really, *really* hard.

Which begs the question: *Why?* Why is controlling our self-stories so hard?

INVISIBLE, TRIGGERED, REPEATING, OH MY!

Controlling your self-stories is so difficult because of a near-impossible set of characteristics stacked against you. By nature (and evolution), self-stories are subconscious, easily triggered, automatic, and habitual. Read that again:

Self-stories are:

- *Subconscious.* Essentially invisible to the human eye.
- *Triggered.* Set off by an event, occurrence, or interaction.
- *Automatic and repeating.* A habit. A well-oiled machine. As seamless as breath.

If you've ever tried to gain control over a habit—like biting your nails, or clearing your throat when you're nervous, or smoking, or saying "like," every other word—then you know how challenging it can be. That little black box of stories that is affecting your results is no different. Here's a closer look at what you're up against.

YOUR SELF-STORIES ARE (MOSTLY) INVISIBLE

Living in New York City during 2020 was an experience—one I am quite certain I won't fully understand until many years from now when time and wisdom will help me piece the story together. As you might imagine, there were several months where our interaction with the outside world consisted solely of walking to an empty Central Park (literally, empty) and watching the world from our street-facing fourth-floor bedroom window.

There are so many stories I could tell, stories I witnessed from that window, pre-pandemic, and beyond. But the one that reappears in my mind as I write this chapter is a story about *rats*.

Yes. I'm afraid rats and self-storytelling are related.

One May evening, warmer temps and the sense of immediate danger subsiding slightly had brought a little more action to the street outside my window. In the dusk light, scattered pairs of people walked the streets, and two young women strolled past Dos Toros, the taco shop directly across from our apartment. They were chatting and laughing—I remember it caught my eye because it looked so *normal*. A complete and amazing contrast to the previous two months.

That moment of calm was quickly shattered when one of the women let out a bloodcurdling shriek. She pointed to the sidewalk, and her friend joined in as they began frantically hopping from one foot to the other in a strange kind of "the floor is lava" dance.

Except it wasn't lava. It was *rats*. The taco shop had put their trash out for collection that night, and as the friends strolled by, the rats had begun their nightly routine of scurrying across the sidewalk to the trash pile, grabbing Mexican takeout for dinner, and scurrying back to their hidden lairs. That evening, the two worlds—the rodent world and the human world—collided, leaving these two unsuspecting friends horrified to catch a glimpse of a truth they'd rather not see: there are rats *everywhere*.

Experts say that at any given moment, there are millions of rats living in the Big Apple. "There is no reliable census," says the *Wall Street Journal* (rats are notorious for not filling out the reporting document), but they are most certainly there.[1] But despite the fact that they may actually outnumber the number of humans in the city, some New Yorkers insist they've never seen one. And I believe them. Why? Because that's the nature of rats. They are under-the-radar experts. Scurrying through grates, infesting nooks and crannies where humans rarely look, they are pretty much left to their own, sometimes destructive devices—even chewing through wires in vehicles, causing thousands of dollars of damage.[2]

But make no mistake. Just because you may be one of the lucky ones who never sees them does not mean they are not there. The rats are always there. Even as Carrie Bradshaw traipsed down pristine sidewalks in her Manolos, a slight camera pan to the left and a swift zoom in would have revealed a whole world of rodents who care little of fashion, despite their sleek fur.

The same is true for our stories. Which is the first reason they are so hard to gain control over. We barely notice they're there.

But they are. Running wild, just below the surface of our consciousness, are our stories. *So* many stories. Stories from elementary school. Stories from that summer with all the cousins. Stories of the times you tried but failed. The bus ride home when a kid made fun of you. The story of that time in high school when, even though you made that epic shot, the team still lost the game. That time you realized a group of parents got together after your daughter's soccer game, and they didn't text you. The story of the time you only missed one word on the spelling test, but that's the only word your dad focused on. The story of the interview you thought went awesome, but when you answered their call, they had decided to "go in a different direction."

Stories from a decade ago, from last century, and last Saturday. From every nook and cranny of the person you were or are or have been or hope to be. These stories scurry around in the vast, untapped space of your unconscious like the rats that run wild and untamed in the city. And like rats chewing the wiring in cars, the reckless abandon of your self-stories can have a significant impact on the conduits of your life—on your happiness, sense of control, and overall fulfillment in life. As Swiss psychologist Carl Jung is purported to have stated: "Until you make the unconscious conscious, it will direct your life, and you will call it Fate."

If there is any hope of taking control of your stories and making significant changes in life, it must start with seeing these mostly invisible stories for what they are.

YOUR SELF-STORIES ARE EASILY TRIGGERED

Have you ever set a certain ringtone on your phone for a particular person or group of people? I have a friend who had a specific ringtone for anyone related to her work. We'll be out with a group of friends for happy hour, and her phone will ring, and without even looking at it, a shadow crosses her face, and her mood turns sour.

Like Pavlov's dogs, the "work" ringtone can send her deep into self-storytelling misery. Though she looks as though she's listening to talk of an upcoming vacation and discussion regarding a new brand of workout gear, my friend, triggered by the ringtone, is drowning in a sea of negative self-stories. The time she was ignored at a morning Stand Up meeting. The time her manager kept calling her even though she was on leave visiting her mother, who was in treatment for breast cancer. The story of the time she totally delivered on a project and her partner took the credit even though he doubted it until the second it was successful (as she knew it would be). The story of the client who called and berated her for a problem that she didn't cause. And if that weren't enough, there are also the stories of her older sister who struck gold right out of college and was now a social media celebrity. And that business someone at her church started and wanted to bring her in on, but she declined, and now the business is booming.

All of that storytelling triggered by a phone call she didn't even pick up.

And, as we just learned, the retelling of those stories happened without her fully realizing they're there. She participated in the vacation discussion, suggesting a restaurant our friend should try while on her trip. She confirmed the new workout brand made the best sports bra ever. All the while being fully tortured by the stories that, like the rats of New York are triggered by the taco shop trash being placed on the sidewalk, were triggered by a ringtone.

If ever Dorothy considered surrendering, could you blame her?

A ringtone is just one example. Triggers come in many shapes and forms. They can be planned events or spontaneous happenings. They can be people. They can be in articles you read, buried in conversations you have, and attached to emotions you feel. The endless opportunities for triggering subconscious, automated self-stories are another reason they are so difficult to control.

YOUR SELF-STORIES ARE AUTOMATIC AND ON REPEAT

Netflix has a feature where, every once in a while, after one episode but before automatically playing the next, a screen pops up to ask: *Are you still watching?*

In normal life, I appreciated that screen. If you didn't answer, Netflix would assume you'd fallen asleep on the couch and wouldn't stream the next episode lest you miss an entire season. (During the pandemic, I'll admit, I felt judged. "Stop asking if I'm still watching! What else am I supposed to be doing?! This is all I've got!")

Storytelling is neurologically "wired-in." It's a habitual, often unconscious, and self-reinforcing process that we repeat over and over. Our self-stories are a lot like binge-watching a show, except without the platform extending the courtesy of checking to see if you're still paying attention to the content. Your brain will play your stories continuously and on repeat as long as you let it, and, like any habit, the more you tell a story, the more neurologically wired in and repeatable it becomes. And, like your physical habits, your story habits can either serve you or keep you stuck where you are. Your habit of going to the gym, for example, can serve you. Your story habit of telling yourself how you're *so terrible* at sticking with things does the opposite, keeping you from going to a gym in the first place.

Self-stories become like well-worn grooves that are easy to slip into and difficult to get out of. And while you may not be completely aware of the repetitive tendencies of your stories, you've certainly seen their effects. You may even recognize some of these:

- The way every new relationship seems to start out great, then turn sour at some point.
- Every time you think you've made a little financial progress and have a few dollars in the bank, something happens to erase it.
- New career and business opportunities never quite seem to materialize.
- Your efforts to make lifestyle changes like eating better or being more active seem to start strong, then sputter and die.

These effects—and so many more—are the impacts of the unattended stories in our life. They're the symptoms of a repeating set of stories we never quite see. They're the results we don't want but always seem to get.

You've likely heard the phrase: "The definition of insanity is doing the same thing over and over and expecting different results." And while I don't disagree, I *do* think the quote oversimplifies the problem. You *know* what not to do. You *know* the thing that you're doing is keeping you from what you want, and you kick yourself each time you do it. Yes, it makes you crazy because if you *know* better, why don't you *do* better? The insanity definition misses the mark by implying that the problem starts with the *doing*. It doesn't. We go crazy because the invisible, habitual, automatic stories we tell ourselves on repeat *lead* to doing the thing that doesn't work.

I get it; my version doesn't look as good on an inspirational-quote magnet. But if you've been driven insane by your behaviors before, this notion alone can change everything.

It isn't the behavior that is holding you back.

It is the hidden story you tell *before* the behavior.

By repeating the same story, we do the same things, and we get the same results as always. The new job remains unapplied for. The new business remains unstarted. The book remains unwritten. The jeans remain too tight. The relationship remains strained. Life stays as status quo. The gap remains uncrossed.

BREAKING THE BAD STORY HABIT

The good news is that any habit can be broken and replaced with a better, more productive one—and that's true of your story habits as well. It's exactly what you're going to do step by step in part II. For now, remember this:

1. If there is an area of your life you wish to change, gaining control over your self-stories is the path to getting there.
2. Self-stories are essentially invisible to the human eye. They're told subconsciously.
3. Self-stories are often triggered by an event, occurrence, or interaction.
4. Once triggered, self-stories are an automatic and repeating habit—a habit that needs to be broken.

Breaking the bad self-story habit requires opportunities for *interruption*. To uncover and stop a negative self-story from chewing through the wires of your self-worth and keep you from getting to the Emerald City. It is possible! There are moments—tip-of-the-iceberg moments—where a story reveals itself, just a little. Those moments, which you'll learn how to identify in chapter 4, offer an opportunity to catch the larger story iceberg, drag it up on the banks of your conscious mind, and start to reshape it into something that serves you.

THERE IS ALWAYS A STORY

In just a few pages, we're going to head into part II, where you'll learn exactly how to reauthor your story from the inside out using a four-part process:

1. Catching your self-storyteller in the act
2. Analyzing a story for its truth and impact in your life
3. Choosing the story to serve you better
4. Installing that story in your brain and life for better results

Whether you're reading this and thinking, "Whoa. This is so me. I have so many stories inside my head," or you're reading this and thinking, "This is a little too far out there for me," make no mistake: *not* telling a story isn't an option.

There is no "no-story" plan. Your brain doesn't work that way. There *are* stories there. And you *are* telling them to yourself whether you know it or not.

Now, if you are at that particular place in your life where you're not facing any gaps, where you've achieved everything you desire, then perhaps yes, you already trained your inner narrator, in which case, I hope this book becomes a confirmation of what exactly you did right. Regardless, self-actualization doesn't mean the absence of stories, but rather the mastery *of* them, and that begins with acknowledging their existence.

The stories are there.

You can either take charge of your stories, or you can let them run your life the way they have been. The choice is yours.

TWO PRINCESSES AND THE STORY THAT SAVED ME

So: about that fall day in New York when I was offered the opportunity I'd been dreaming of, and promptly went home and cried on the floor in the bathroom.

I feel it's important you know that I am not a "cry on the bathroom floor" kinda girl.

In fact, that afternoon was the first and only time, and I fully blame the intensity of the self-story avalanche for that behavior.

However, it was there on the bathroom floor that I found some clarity.

Sure, there were indeed plenty of stories of mom-fails—that's pretty much what parenting is. Getting it wrong in big ways and small ways and hoping your kids will learn from your mistakes and do better when the next generation comes kicking and screaming into the world.

But if there were plenty of stories of how I'd failed, weren't there also—if I looked for them—plenty of stories of winning? Stories of when the particular way I parent or the kind of mom *I* am and even the work I do actually *served* my children and made me a *good* mom?

It turns out, focusing on finding one of those stories, even just for a minute, with my back against the bathtub, yielded some powerful results. One of my favorites was from just a few years before.

Two Princesses and the Big Castle

The story happened when I was a couple of years into my business and, even then, struggling with whether or not I was a "good mother." The travel, the stress, the ambition—I was struggling with the fact that my work meant opting out of homework and spelling tests and running the kids back and forth from activities. I struggled to participate in group chats with the other moms as I tried to figure out sales and scale, marketing and management, all at the same time.

One afternoon I was home with my daughter, who was about three at the time, and we were building something on her bedroom floor out of blocks. I was distracted, going through the motions of putting one block on top of another but not actively *building* anything, and then my daughter spoke.

"Mama," she said in a tone I recognized—it was the tone you use when someone isn't paying attention, and they should be. "We are building a castle." She motioned to the haphazard pile of blocks. I immediately came back to reality. "Oh yes!" I said as if I could tell it was a castle—a castle with some serious architectural issues, but a castle all the same. I picked up a couple of blocks and began working on one of the towers.

"And this is *our* castle, Mama," she continued as she put one block on top of another. "We live in this castle because we are two princesses." I wish there were a way to insert into this book the way her sweet little girl voice said "princesses," but alas, there is not. I remember thinking what a beautiful thing it was to be seen as a princess by your daughter.

"*And*," my daughter said with emphasis. She stopped abruptly, put down the bricks she had been holding, and looked me in the eye, her sandy blonde curls wild around her round little face. I had always called her a force of nature (my mother had called her karma), and the fierceness in her gaze as she looked at me confirmed that neither of us was wrong.

"And it's a *big* castle, Mama. Because we are two princesses who go . . . to . . . *work!*" She nodded her head slightly on that last word, feeling it deserved a physical expression of punctuation, and then went right back to building.

I replayed that moment in my mind that Thursday afternoon in October sitting on the bathroom floor. I allowed *that* story to fully take hold. I understood that, yes, while there were things that I was going to miss, while our life might look a little different than the families around us, it didn't automatically mean it was wrong. Or that I was doing a bad job.

Maybe, I realized, by being true to myself and pursuing my passion, I was teaching my daughter to dream bigger, to build whatever castle she wanted, to go *for* it and go *through* it, and know that the people who love her will love her no matter what.

I called my agent.

"I'm in," I said. "But I need to leave Saturday morning instead. I'm going to pick my kids up from school tomorrow and have dinner together."

It remains one of the most important *yes* moments of my career.

A *yes* that almost didn't happen because my stories were telling me *no*.

I am so grateful I chose to tell myself a better one.

THE SELF-STORY CHOICE

Within each of us are millions of stories. Small events, big tragedies, things we can barely remember, and others we'll never forget. And yes, a lot of the stories aren't great. There are times when we were betrayed, or we betrayed someone else. There are stories of injustice and outcomes that were unfair or consequences that were undeserved. There are stories of abandonment, of foolish mistakes, of arrogance. There are stories of people rejecting us or making fun of us or shaming us or treating us as though we were less than. I mean, thinking back to sixth grade alone could leave you with stories stacked up as tall as a skyscraper.

I am not saying those stories aren't there. In fact, I am saying they *definitely* are and, if you haven't done so, it's time to acknowledge them.

What I am *also* saying is that there are skyscrapers of positive stories, *too*. Of times you beat the odds. Stories of being loved and loving in return. There are stories of people believing in you, cheering for you, and of you believing in yourself. They don't have to be big. As the participants in the project I mentioned above were surprised to discover, and as you'll learn, too, some stories last a moment, are a few sentences long, and yet, there is something about the emotion behind them that, when retold, gives a surge of positive energy.

That "story" piece of the process between Event and Response is owned by *you*. It is your choice. Choosing what story or stories you tell yourself can change your response, which in turn changes your results. Put that on repeat, and suddenly, your life can look wholly different.

While you don't get a choice in whether or not stories are being told—like it or not, the story is happening—the good news is that *the choice of which stories you tell is entirely yours*. Because while there are certainly stories that keep you stuck, that make you feel heavy, and cause you to wonder if you'll ever cross the great divide, there are also stories that can set you free. There are stories that can propel you forward. There are stories that can lift you up and over the challenges, stories that can break through the barriers. Yes, I realize as I write this that it sounds like there should be inspirational music playing in the background, and you know what? *There should* be.

Because the science, research, and evidence from each of our own experiences in this difficult, wonderful, story-filled world point to one powerful thing:

If you can change your story, you can change your life.

PART II

THE SELF-STORYTELLING PROCESS

Reconstructing Your Inner Voice

CATCH

Identifying Your Invisible Stories

I've always thought the sound that you make is just the tip of the iceberg,
like the person that you see physically is just the tip of the iceberg as well.

—YO-YO MA

A significant portion of my junior year of high school was dedicated to the movie *Titanic*. I saw it with my girlfriends, I saw it with the boy I was hoping would be my boyfriend, we recreated it for a Spanish 3 assignment, and we danced to it at prom (okay, *I* danced to it at prom—my sort-of-boyfriend didn't want to dance). The music, the tragedy, and most of all, the love story. Now, almost twenty-five years later (yes, that math is correct), I find myself much less interested in the love story and much more fascinated by how a ship hurtling toward certain doom and unable to change course is an uncomfortably apt metaphor for adult life.

Icebergs in the real world are large chunks of ice that break off from glaciers and free-float in the ocean. Do not let the description deceive you—these icebergs in no way resemble colorful, happy inner tubes drifting down the lazy river at a fancy resort. Icebergs are enormous. Although we'll never know the exact measurements of the iceberg that took out the *Titanic*, it is estimated that it may have been up to four hundred feet long and one hundred feet high. Huge.[1]

Which begs the question:

How was it possible they didn't know it was there?

How, after all the effort, all the attention to detail, all the meticulous engineering, did the *Titanic* miss something as obvious as a mass of ice that big? And while there are some theories about solar storms interrupting magnetic navigation, the reality is that while a giant mass of ice in an otherwise empty ocean would be pretty easy to spot and avoid, 90 percent of an iceberg's mass is hidden below the waterline, all but invisible to the naked eye.[2]

Imagine that. Something with the ability to send an invincible ship to the bottom of the sea in under three hours but that is essentially *invisible*. And while the story of the *Titanic* is certainly a tragic one, this is not actually about a ship that sank over a century ago.

This is about you.

When thinking about life, regardless of your approach for creating it—maybe you're an obsessive goal-setter or committed to meditation and manifestation, or maybe you're someone who prefers to throw your chips in the air and see where they fall—there is often that sense that, while it isn't always as abrupt or aggressive as a mass of ice tearing a hole in the hull of a gigantic ship, there is something lurking under the surface that is keeping you anchored and unable to reach your intended destination.

You're not alone. Some 80 percent of people admit to feeling stuck in their routines.[3] Less than 20 percent keep their resolutions.[4] More than 50 percent are unhappy at work.[5] We're all facing gaps between where we are and where we want to be, either in love or business or health or money, and we can't quite figure out why. What is holding us back? What is keeping us frozen in place?

The answer for humans is not unlike the answer that sank the unsinkable ship: an enormous mass, just out of view. But for us, this mass isn't made of ice. It's made of stories.

ICEBERG MOMENTS: SIGNS OF THE STORIES 20,000 LEAGUES UNDER THE SEA

Let's take a moment to revisit the big idea from the previous chapter—that stories are determining the results you get in life:

WHAT REALLY HAPPENS
EVENT → STORY → RESPONSE → RESULT

Stories are inserting themselves into our lives, changing how we think, feel, and act. The trouble is that the story part of this whole thing isn't easy to see! While you can usually see the events that trigger your stories, and you can see your responses and the results you get, the story itself—the thing that's really creating your life—is far trickier. It's a mostly hidden iceberg, like this:

No matter which way you turn your ship, the stories are there, overlapping and crisscrossing the latitude and longitude lines of your life. For each of the crossroads in your life where you want to say yes, but say no, there's an iceberg for that. Every time you've turned down an invitation? Iceberg. When you didn't apply for something because you thought you weren't qualified? There's an iceberg for that, too. When you kept quiet in a meeting with your peers, iceberg. When you skipped your workout: Ahoy! Iceberg!

For every time you've given up too early, shied away, or taken the wrong path, there's been a near-invisible force at work. If you held your breath, plunged beneath the glacial waters of your consciousness, and had the courage to open your eyes, you would see an icy castle of stories that are holding you back.

If there is any hope of making significant changes in life, the proverbial "polar plunge" is required. Change starts with seeing these stories in the first place.

But how do you catch an invisible story?

Fortunately, much like icebergs, our story-masses are not *completely* invisible. There is hope for catching them on your radar and navigating around them. Sometimes, if just for a moment, a story protrudes above the surface of your consciousness and leaves ripples in the water that, if you're paying attention, you can see and that reveal the larger story-mass beneath. The storyteller in you may be working in secret, beneath the level of your awareness, but inevitably the work of the inner teller pops its head above the surface, if just for a moment.

These brief instants when a story at work reveals itself are what I call "iceberg moments," and they are an opportunity.

Iceberg moments are clues to your self-stories. They might be small. They may be fleeting and hard to spot, but they are clues nonetheless.

And catching them is where changing your life begins.

The rest of this chapter has a singular goal: to help you with the first step of this method—catching your self-stories in the act. To be able to identify the ripples in the, let's face it, sometimes rough waters of life, as a signal to look below the surface to see what's there.

You've heard of taking control of your life; it starts here. It's time to set up your radar so the next time you encounter one of your icebergs, it doesn't rip a hole in your life and sink the ship while you're busy rearranging deck chairs.

"ICEBERG, DEAD AHEAD, SIR!": CATCHING YOUR SELF-STORY AT WORK

Meet Amie.

Amie works for a financial start-up company. From her home in Arizona, she remotely manages a customer service team that is based in the Philippines. One Monday morning she received word that there had been a massive blowup during a call between one of her customer-service reps, Joseph Scott, and a customer.

Apparently, the customer had abruptly asked, "Is your real name even Joseph Scott?" As policy, all Amie's team members in the Philippines use American names in an effort to make communication easier. When Joseph Scott told the customer this, the customer began to yell, calling the employee a liar, and saying he could no longer trust the company.

It was an emotionally charged moment for everyone. And now, it was Amie's job to sort it out. Amie would listen to the call to get an objective look at how exactly things went off the rails, then speak to the customer and, finally, Joseph Scott.

Now, Amie is no stranger to calls gone bad. These things happen in her work, and she's good at her job. But as she played back the tape, a sinking feeling began to consume her. And the longer she listened, the worse she started to feel.

"It threw off my week," she said. "I was getting so nervous. It was eating at me in the pit of my stomach. My mind was spinning."

It had nothing to do with the actual content of the call or what actions were required to resolve the situation. It was pretty much a case study pulled right out of the policies and procedures handbook. So, what, then, was causing Amie to have such an extreme adverse reaction?

"Then I thought, it's the stories."

Amie was a participant in the group I took through this book's method over the course of six weeks. Each Monday, we had a group session via Zoom where I explained each step of the method and gave them assignments. And then, as I mentioned previously, I met with each participant individually to discuss their personal self-storytelling journey and give them individualized guidance for using the power of the stories within them.

In our first individual session, I gave each participant a strategy for identifying the signs of a hidden story at work—for seeing their iceberg moments. After years of practicing this method myself, I've found there are four types of iceberg moments: *verbal*, *physiological*, *behavioral*, and *emotional*. Each is a clue to a deeper story at work.

VERBAL ICEBERG MOMENTS

At the end of the first group session, I asked the participants to pay attention throughout the week to see if they could identify clues in their language that might mark their own verbal iceberg statements. To be clear, they aren't always verbalized *aloud*. Sometimes these statements are "spoken" inside your own head.

That week, each participant came to me with a different list of things they said to themselves on a regular basis. Here are just a few of them—perhaps some may sound familiar:

- I'll never live up to my potential.
- I need to be careful of my injury (so I shouldn't work out).
- I don't matter.
- I am unlucky.
- I am just lucky.
- I'm failing my kids.
- I'm bad with money.
- Nothing works out for me.

- I'm not meant for success.
- I'm a bad father.
- I'm not good enough.
- I'm not worthy.
- I'm too old.
- I'm not successful outside my comfort zone.
- I'm only capable of doing this much.
- If I haven't done it by now, I'll never do it.
- I always play it safe.
- I don't have enough money.
- I'm not a salesperson.
- I'm too busy.
- I'm a failure.

For hours, I sat across from people in their living rooms, their back patios, their makeshift offices they built in the closet or in the basement, or in the shed in their backyard and watched as they read aloud a list of the terrible things they think about themselves, a litany of phrases they say to themselves on a weekly, daily, even hourly basis. Each time, after they shared their list, I asked them what it was like to identify those statements.

Many of them were surprised at how cruel the statements were. "I can't believe I say this to myself." Others were surprised and disgusted at how rampant these beliefs were. "I caught myself saying this to myself at least fifty times yesterday." Many shook their heads as they looked at the piece of paper in front of them—it was written in their handwriting, these were words from their own minds, and yet it was as if the phrases came from somewhere else. Some unseen place. And though they desperately wanted these statements not to be true, they believed them. And they hated it.

The good news? Becoming aware of those sentences is the beginning of the end of self-sabotage and limiting beliefs and a powerful step toward freedom.

I have found that verbal clues are often the best place to start because they're the most common and the easiest to identify.

I Am / I Am Not Statements

Also known as belief statements, these phrases are the most obvious indicator of a self-story at work. Whenever you find yourself with that thought in your head that confidently says you *are* or *are not* something, that's an iceberg moment. Phrases that include *always* or *never* are also dead giveaways to a self-story working against you. There is also the half-sister—that you *can* or *cannot* do something—and the close cousin that you *couldn't* or *wouldn't* be able to do something.

If you're lucky, you'll hear yourself say the words aloud and, now that you've read this paragraph, you'll be able to catch it. However, it's more likely these statements are only uttered between your ears, never aloud. And quite possibly in a snarky, condescending tone, or one that is aggravatingly cool, calm, and fully convincing. (Believe me, I know icebergs.) Regardless of the tone or volume, as soon as you hear one of those phrases above, set off the alarms. It's all hands on deck, iceberg ahead!

Well-Dressed Excuses

Meet Maggie.
Maggie knew she needed to make some changes to her lifestyle. After spending her entire youth as a ballerina, then an avid hiker, an adventure seeker, and a novice runner, she felt bogged down by old injuries and her health was heading in a direction she knew wasn't good. Despite her best intentions, she couldn't seem to get back on track.

Suspicious this might be a self-storytelling issue, she took out her binoculars and started scanning the surface of her consciousness for tips of icebergs—belief statements that could be indicators of a deeper issue. It didn't take long before she found a few. However, while she expected to find statements that were ugly and obvious, what she *got* were statements that actually sounded "good." The challenge was figuring out if these statements were friends or foes.

Maggie discovered a classic iceberg statement move, one that makes them tricky to identify; they can take the form of "well-dressed excuses." On the surface, they sound great. They sound wise. They sound aligned with a life well lived and, in some cases, they are so virtuous that to question them would be downright disrespectful. For example, I knew another woman who desperately wanted to fall in love and start a family, but she was really struggling to meet *anyone*, much less *the* one. It was frustrating, to say the least. But if you were to ask her how she was meeting people, she would say she wasn't really putting herself out there. "God will send me the right person," was her mantra. Now, that sounds pretty good. I mean, you can't argue with God. But she was literally not talking to any men, ever. She was waiting for God to deliver him to her doorstep. That meant that unless the FedEx guy was single and interested, she was in trouble.

Here are a couple of Maggie's well-dressed excuses:

- *"I can't fix what I'm born with."* It's true; we all face a set of genetic circumstances. Embedded within the twisting strands of our DNA are a certain set of realities. (Knees, for example. I have long wanted a different set of knees. Mine are perfectly functional, but I would prefer a pair that, when in great shape, look like Carrie Underwood's knees. It turns out, however, that no matter what shape I'm in, my knees are always going to resemble Grandma Phyllis's knees.) After a more thorough examination of this statement, Maggie realized that while there *was* some truth in the statement, it was a well-dressed tip of an iceberg of stories that were keeping her stuck. Why try so hard if you can't fix what you're born with?
- *"You only live once!"* This was another statement that, on the surface, sounds awesome. Take more risks! Do the things! It's the

acronym of the century; when you're YOLO'ing, you can do no wrong. Except that for Maggie, only living once meant, "Sure, I'll have that pie! Yes to another cocktail! Why not stay out way too late and skip anything productive the next day?! YOLO!" The well-dressed excuse sounded good but made change a lot more challenging.

If you find yourself giving a logical reason for making a choice or engaging in a behavior that is contrary to your ambitions, regardless of how good it sounds, you could be staring your iceberg in the eye and not even know it. Well-dressed excuses may sound good, but they are actually red flares indicating your ship is headed for disaster.

PHYSIOLOGICAL ICEBERG MOMENTS

I recently interviewed Alexi Pappas, Olympian and author of the fantastic book *Bravey*. During our fascinating conversation, she mentioned something a trainer once told her. It turns out we have the most nerves in our face, hands, and stomachs—it's the reason our stomachs "turn" when we're nervous. On one occasion, while working through an injury, Alexi's physio asked her if she had noticed any changes on her face in the days and weeks leading up to the injury. As a matter of fact, she had. She had a strange, unexplained little splotch under her eye that looked like a sunburn. It disappeared almost as quickly as it came, but it wasn't nothing—it was a signal that she was pushing too hard.

The connection between the body and mind has long been studied (we'll talk more about it in chapter 9) and if you pay attention, the body can send clues of an iceberg ahead. Think of the physical quirks you have when you get anxious or nervous. Perhaps you're a nail-biter. One of the women in my research said her husband commented that she clears her throat in a strange way whenever she receives an email from her boss. A sure physiological sign that

I'm coming up against a big iceberg is my lower back. There have been several key moments in my life when I've been reaching for another level only to be grounded by inexplicable back pain. I've had an MRI; I've been on medication. I went to physical therapy, where they told me the reason my back was giving me so much trouble was because I had my kids close together, and I'm short. (For the record, I'm 5'4", and I know for a fact there are shorter women who have had two babies in the span of seventeen minutes; mine were separated by seventeen months.) Fortunately, I had a friend suggest that maybe the problem wasn't my back but my head. Thankfully, I resisted the urge to punch him and discovered that pain in my lower back is indeed a billboard-sized sign of stories that need to be attended to.

To be clear, this is not a replacement for medical treatment. It is important to consult with a physician. I find it fascinating how closely our bodies and minds work together. Pay attention in case yours is trying to tell you something.

BEHAVIORAL ICEBERG MOMENTS

These might be less obvious to you, but they're no less revealing. That sudden urge to clean the kitchen? The email inbox you suddenly *must* check even though you aren't expecting any messages? The text you suddenly feel the need to send? The social media app you need to scroll? The urge to eat, smoke, or distract yourself with your favorite show? They can all be signs that a self-story is running rampant and unattended in the background. Even things that seem like positive habits—exercising or working—can be signs that a story is lurking, and you're unconsciously trying to avoid it. We've all heard stories of the person who throws themselves into work when things are challenging at home and eventually their family crumbles. Or the young woman who attends multiple fitness classes a day in an effort to fight off the inner stories telling her she's not worthy.

I've found this single question helpful: What habits do I have that are the opposite of what I want? If you want to lose ten pounds but order pizza multiple times a week and devour at least half of it yourself, why is that? The answer to *that* question will lead you closer to the iceberg in your way.

EMOTIONAL ICEBERG MOMENTS

Fear. Dread. Shame. Embarrassment. Jealousy. The emotions we love to hate are also the tips of story icebergs. Do you ever get a rush of emotion that seems to come from nowhere? Perhaps you feel suddenly irritated or sad in the middle of a conversation or after reading something on your phone. Maybe your heart races a little, or your mood suddenly darkens. I call it a UFE—an unidentified flying emotion—that feeling you can't quite put your finger on.

For example, I was out for a walk one morning with Michael at a time when the news of the day was the rollout of the COVID-19 vaccine. Michael was following the story and would keep me updated, always with excitement in his voice. On this particular day, I realized I *wasn't* feeling excited about the vaccine, and every time he mentioned it, I felt that uncomfortable, UFE sensation. Knowing that this was the sign of a self-story at work, I went looking for the iceberg beneath and found it almost immediately.

It was the fall of 2010. I was pregnant with my first child and I had a doctor's appointment. I remembered the exact room I was sitting in (the one on the north side of the building), what I was wearing (a pale pink maternity tunic), and that my doctor wasn't there that day. The woman who *was* there had coarse reddish-brown hair and glasses and asked if I was getting my flu shot during my visit. I stuttered slightly in responding.

"Actually, I hadn't considered it," I said. "Could it wait until my next appointment?" After all, I'd researched just about everything else that went into my body during pregnancy—cheese and three-times-washed lettuce included—it seemed strange not to look into this a little or at least mention it to my husband.

The woman then proceeded to berate me, making me feel as though I were a murderous baby-hater. "I am going to leave this room," she said, "and when I walk back in, you'd better tell me to give you the shot."

I remember shaking. I remember sweating. I remember feeling confused and scared and attacked. And when the woman returned, syringe in hand, I accepted the shot, she gave it to me, and, right or wrong, I went home feeling coerced and not fully comfortable with what had just happened.

That was it. That was the event, the story that was silently replaying in my subconscious and the source of that UFE. It was this story that was emerging during our vaccine discussions. With it now out in the light, I was able to, in terms of the current situation at hand, move forward with more clarity and awareness.

Emotions are there for a reason, and they're often sitting on top of a much bigger set of stories just out of view.

AMIE'S ICEBERG MOMENTS

"Then I thought, it's the stories."

As Amie prepared for her call with the angry customer, the clues to her hidden iceberg weren't hard to spot. The feelings of anxiousness, the spinning mind? Those were emotional signs. The beating heart, the gnawing at the pit of her stomach? Physiological clues. And, above it all, with just a little excavation, a verbal statement emerged: "Whenever I have to deal with irrational people, I shut down." A crystal-clear iceberg moment.

As Amie dug into her story, more of the iceberg beneath began to show itself. In particular, she found a story of an incident from almost eight years earlier when an irrational man had bullied her in the workplace and turned her colleagues against her.

"It was a traumatic moment that I've never forgotten," she said. "It was six months of my life." Listening to the call with Joseph Scott and hearing the angry customer triggered the old story of the irrational bully at work. To Amie's brain, those two men were one and the same and her mind was doing anything it could to keep Amie safe.

Having been through several sessions with me, Amie was able to catch the tip of the iceberg and dip below the water level to see more of the story beneath. The hard part, however, was knowing what to do next. As she told her husband, "I have to focus on the positive stories. But I can't think of any."

Her husband had no such problem. He reminded her of many other times she had confronted people who treated her poorly. The times she had ended relationships that were irrational and was able to handle them in a completely rational, effective way. Amie clearly *had* dealt with irrational people many times and done it successfully. She just couldn't see it at first; that one traumatic story from her past kept playing loudest.

As Amie prepared for her meeting with Joseph Scott and the angry customer, she replayed those supportive stories from her past.

"It worked!" she told me. "I was able to go calmly into the call, and it ended up being just fine."

IT'S NOT ALL BAD

We signed the lease on our first New York City apartment at the end of March 2018. We started buying furniture and moving it in in April but didn't officially move in until August. Some of my favorite memories are of the few weekends between April and August when we came to visit. They remind me of those intangible moments between wake and sleep when a good dream suspends.

One of those weekends was in early June, when the city was flawlessly warm and welcoming. It was that weekend that we met our upstairs neighbor, a woman in her nineties named Danuta, who invited Michael and me and our two children up for tea, milk, and treats.

We had planned a quick visit; we were there for two hours. Her apartment was one hundred degrees. We almost broke the antique teapot three different times. My daughter drank a gallon of milk and is probably lactose sensitive. And none of it mattered. Danuta's stories were addictive. Her husband was a Polish diplomat. They'd met in DC and moved to NYC. He had passed away twenty years earlier. And while she didn't tell us *all* her stories, one thing was clear: Danuta had been through it all. She had seen things, lived things, survived things we hadn't even read about, never mind experienced. Though her frame was small and her skin was fragile, Danuta was mighty. Even our kids knew we had encountered someone special.

You can imagine, then, the mix of emotions I felt in March of 2020, not quite two years after that warm June day, when I looked out my fourth-floor window onto the deserted pandemic streets of New York City to see none other than our fifth-floor neighbor walking home with groceries from the store several blocks away.

Clearly, Danuta was in the category of people most at risk of coronavirus. Everything we had heard, read, and seen said she should be holed up in her apartment, terrified to leave. And yet there she was, walking down the street as confident and interesting as she'd ever been—only now with new accessories: a mask, gloves, and, one could only assume, a tiny little bottle of hand sanitizer. While the rest of the world was cowering in fear, Danuta was grocery shopping. And though she wasn't saying it aloud, I felt as though I could *hear* the stories she was telling herself from my windowsill. They added up to *I've been through worse.*

The experts will tell you her behavior was irresponsible. And while that may be true, the story expert will tell you that, sometimes, there are statements and beliefs that serve you. Maybe you were always told and believed that you are a people-person, and that belief has allowed you to network your way into incredible places. Maybe you were always the one given the ball at the buzzer during high school basketball games and, nine times out of ten, you made the shot and those stories have led to the belief that you work great under pressure. Not all iceberg tips are bad. Sometimes there are icebergs that move us forward, that encourage us to take risks that others wouldn't and therefore reap rewards that others won't. Perhaps it's better to think of these as small tropical islands. Places of sun and joy and respite on our journey. Your positive stories are there, waiting for you.

HEADING BENEATH THE WAVES

Identifying your tip-of-the-iceberg moments does two important things. First of all, it slows or ideally stops the automatic storytelling from running wild just beneath the surface of your awareness. It makes the unconscious conscious.

Second, it allows you to move into the second phase of the self-storytelling method.

Amie's success wasn't just about catching the iceberg moment. Iceberg statements, while powerful in and of themselves, aren't the whole story; they're just the tip. The rest is largely hidden in the depths, stirring currents in your brain and acting as an anchor to keep you stuck right where you are.

Amie was able to go further—to analyze the story beneath the surface and then to find a better set of stories to replace the one that didn't serve her. That's exactly what we'll do in the chapters ahead.

Now that you know how to catch a self-story at work, it's time to, like Amie, start exploring what stories really lie beneath the waves.

ANALYZE

Putting Your Inner Story Under the Magnifying Glass

*The storytelling mind is a factory that churns out true stories
when it can, but will manufacture lies when it can't.*

—JONATHAN GOTTSCHALL

In the previous chapter, we learned that, if you look, you can spot the subtle signs of a story at work—tiny glimpses of the larger story-iceberg beneath the surface.

Finding those clues is an essential beginning. Until you can point to something and say, "Ah. Yes. I see what's going on here," you'll never be able to interrupt the unconscious story process long enough to change it. But as with most problems, pointing at them doesn't solve them. Pointing is just a first step. What comes next is to *go below*—to analyze the iceberg beneath the surface so you can begin to choose differently.

EVERYDAY ICEBERGS

Imagine, for example, that you have trouble speaking up at meetings. Each time you think you have something to offer, you second guess yourself and stay silent. Your conscious self might feel silly for this behavior. *It's just a meeting*, you tell yourself. *It's nothing*.

Your inner storyteller, however, doesn't find anything silly about it. It just sees a *risk*. Long ago, rejection by your tribe truly *was* a life-or-death problem. Back when it really *did* take a village to survive, being kicked out of yours meant certain death, and that legacy is still with you and it sets off a familiar cascade of events. The situation collides with a story, the story creates a particular response, and the response leads to a result; or in this case you're in a meeting, you want to contribute but you don't, and you leave the meeting frustrated that your voice never gets heard.

Now, you're no fool. You know your habit of holding back at meetings is a problem. You've already been passed over for several promotions and it will continue to hold you back unless you figure this thing out. You've read a few personal development books and even spoken with an executive coach, both of which suggested positive self-talk and affirmations as a solution.

Willing to try anything, you start by talking some sense into yourself:

Okay, self. That was just a meeting. There's nothing to be afraid of. These people respect you. That's why you're there. No one is going to think less of you if you share your idea. No one is going to point their finger and laugh—this is a professional environment. In fact, you are doing them a disservice by not speaking up. We can't let this happen again.

This is a typical and rational approach to dealing with fear. Just as we might tell a friend who's afraid of flying that it's "safer than driving," we tell ourselves that "there's nothing to be afraid of here." It's a valiant effort, but it rarely works. Being told not to be anxious because it's irrational isn't helpful. When you're nervous about speaking up, you already *know* that nothing truly terrible can happen from a few stammers or a bad suggestion. But self-talk doesn't stop you from staying quiet, so you switch to positive affirmations.

Every morning on the drive to work, you chant into the empty vehicle these phrases:

You are valuable.
You have good ideas.
You are a confident person who speaks up.

You belong here.
I like my hair. I like my haircuts.*

Feeling good, you attend the next meeting and . . . (drum roll) . . . you don't speak up and the whole process starts over again. Why does this happen? Well, while positive self-talk and affirmations may address the tip of the iceberg, remember that that is only about 10 percent of what is actually there. What you're up against is actually much bigger and broader than you could have ever imagined and comprises a lifetime of—you guessed it—stories.

LURKING IN THE DEEP BLUE SEA

Below the surface of your consciousness are archival memories of actual events that occurred over the course of your lifetime. These events, much like individual snowflakes that have compacted into a massive berg, are what strangle your voice and keep you quiet.

Maybe you're the youngest in a family of five and though you frequently met for family meetings to discuss where to go next on vacations, your older siblings always got to share first so by the time they got around to your idea, the decision had already been made (*your opinion doesn't matter*). Or by the time you graduated from high school, it was old news. You distinctly remember the pomp and circumstance when your brother graduated—the many-folding-tables-long spread of catered food, the crowds of people swarming the house and spilling out into the front yard, and the pile of gifts that overtook the living room. And then, just six years later for your graduation, you got a balloon, ham-and-cheese sandwiches, and a smattering of friends, neighbors, and a random cousin who you're pretty sure was filling the pockets of his oversized flannel with ham sandwiches and leaving a trail of cheese

---

* A reference to a super old viral video on YouTube of a little girl giving herself a big hype session standing on her bathroom counter.

slices everywhere he went because he was lactose intolerant (*you don't matter*). Or that time you were in college and had to work on a dreaded group project for ancient philosophy. You very distinctly remember sitting in the library at a table in the back corner at midnight two nights before the presentation was due suggesting to the group that you reenact Plato's allegory of the cave, each of you playing a different prisoner, to maximize creativity points, but the group flatly declined, and your grade suffered as a result (*even your good ideas aren't worth listening to*).

Of course, it seems silly that you would remember these instances at all; they're so small. And yet, now that you think about it, you could describe each of these moments with a shocking amount of detail. The chairs, sofa, and coffee table in the room where "family meetings" were held. You can remember the weather on the day of your makeshift graduation party and the grease-soaked box top of the $8.00 pizza your group had delivered to the back entrance of the library.

Just because a) you never really think about these moments and b) you're *definitely* never asked about them doesn't mean that these memories are random, *nor* are they insignificant. In fact, these instances, these *stories* and many, many more have all been carefully collected, curated, and compacted by your subconscious into a gigantic, unseen threat to everything you've ever desired.

No wonder positive self-talk doesn't work. No wonder affirmations feel futile. Remember, the belief is just the tip of the iceberg. *I'm not good enough. My opinion doesn't matter.* It's like if the crew on the *Titanic*, after seeing the tip of the iceberg protruding from the water, pulled up beside it, lit a match, tossed it at the enormous glacial mass, and wiped their hands. Crisis averted.

There is much more below the surface level of awareness—a lifetime of stories that, unlike the snowflakes of an iceberg that can't be separated from one another, are preserved and exist in their full individual form.

This is what is propping up your limiting beliefs.

This is what you're up against.

Dealing with *this* is what this chapter is all about.

Once you catch your self-stories in the act by spotting the belief, the next step is one of excavation and analysis. The only way you can change your life is by fully understanding, in all its frozen glory, the iceberg that keeps thwarting your voyage. In order to do that we will first address what makes a story stick and second, the six essential questions to ask yourself to get a full analysis of your personal story catalog.

That being said . . . I feel like I should warn you: icebergs can get weird.

I HAD NO IDEA THAT WAS THERE

Catching glimpses of subconscious stories at work, putting a finger on limiting beliefs, and stripping well-dressed excuses to reveal the naked truth can be an awkward sort of revelation. There really *are* stories there. And once you start looking, they are everywhere! Anytime I take someone through Step One and into Step Two they say, "I can't believe I remember that."

Where things always get interesting is when we look just below the surface. If the statement is just the tip of the iceberg, what exactly was down below propping it up and why? The participants in my research group, for example, were shocked by the stories they found.

- One woman remembered the day they got weighed in fifth grade, and she weighed the most, even more than the boys. She remembered exactly what she was wearing, right down to the Michael Jordan T-shirt and high-tops.
- One woman could recite back word for word the email a potential client had written her to explain why he was hiring someone else. She remembered exactly where she was sitting when she read it.

- One man remembered with flawless detail a particular night on a camping trip where his father and cousins left him waiting by the fire while they went into the forest to gather more wood and didn't return for what felt like a lifetime.
- One woman remembered the time in elementary school when she was so excited because she only made one mistake on her math test, and yet when she showed her father, he yelled at her for getting one wrong. She remembered the exact spot in the hallway where she stood and the exact chair he sat in while he yelled at her.

And these were just a handful of the stories that came up, each of them propping up beliefs like, "I've always been heavy," "I'm not very good at my job," "I need to prove my value," "I'm not good enough," or as was the case in the example of speaking up in a meeting, "It's best just to keep quiet."

That will likely be your first reaction as well. Whether you're someone who remembers the birthdays of everyone you've ever met and their favorite kind of pie, or you can't remember where you put your wallet *ever*, you'll be amazed at all the stories that are hovering just beyond the fringes of your awareness.

This shouldn't come as a surprise, however; after all, stories are what stick and the participants in my group were experiencing this firsthand. The challenge they now faced was to understand *why*? In a lifetime that may be filled with *millions* of stories, what made these so memorable? Why had the one moment at a school dance remained so vivid while a thousand others were lost to time? Why did one comment from a colleague in a single meeting linger like a ghost, while so many other hours spent in meetings had left almost zero impression?

That is a similar question to the one I asked in *Stories That Stick*. And while in that book the context was focused on stories told outwardly in business, the *answer* applies here, to the stories we tell ourselves. Because, as I've always said, we are powerful storytellers by nature. Our self-stories effortlessly include the components research has indicated make stories stay.

WHAT MAKES A STORY STICK?

In 2018, my team sought to understand, without a doubt, what made a story stick. What made the difference between a story that sold a lot of products and one that didn't? What stories resonated with people, and which ones fell flat? Our research tested four story components to determine their effect on the impact of the message.

- Identifiable characters
- Authentic emotion
- A significant moment
- Specific details

Our research showed that a message that contained only one of the components performed better than a message with none of the components. Additionally, the more components the message contained, the more appealing the story became. In addition to explaining a story's effectiveness in business, these components help us understand why the stories we tell ourselves are so effortlessly powerful. We naturally *include* these components subconsciously. They are part of what makes us such great storytellers by nature. Every compelling story we craft contains these pieces.

Identifiable Characters

Sometimes the character in the story is *you*. You as a child. You as a young adult, a grown adult, an experienced adult. While some of it is certainly a blur, there are slices of time where you can remember exactly who you were and what you were like. What your dreams were, what games you liked to play, the things you were good at or wanted to be good at. You can remember risks you took or passed on. Even as a passive character in a particular story, an observer of an event instead of a participant, you can still remember your experience.

In addition to the many versions of ourselves in our stories, there is, of course, an endless supply of other characters. The immediate family members or distant relatives, best friends or worst enemies, important coaches or colleagues—the cast of characters we remember spans all types of random interactions. Participants in the project for this book could remember the first and last names of kids they went to elementary school with. They remembered old neighbors they rarely talked to and grocery store workers they haven't seen in years. If you want to lift up a small corner of your memory, just ask one character-based question like, "Who were some of the people who worked with me at my very first job?" You'll be shocked at the people your brain has been carrying around.

Authentic Emotion

The thing all of these characters have in common is that they made you *feel* something. Something good, something bad, but either way, you experienced emotion. You've no doubt heard the famous quote often attributed to Maya Angelou, "People will forget what you said, people will forget what you did, but people will never forget how you made them feel." Authentic emotion is that quote in action, and it is perhaps the most important component in our self-stories.

One day, shortly after I moved to Arizona without knowing a soul, I was putting gas in my car before driving to California in hopes of finding a job. My hair was a mess, I was sweating because it was Arizona and I was outside, and a kind-looking gentleman at the pump next to mine said, "Excuse me, miss, I just want to tell you, you are very beautiful." Then he smiled, got in his car, and drove away. That was it. No follow-up. No cheesy pickup line.

Why would that compliment stand out above the rest? It's not the only compliment I've ever received. And the exchange didn't even span thirty seconds. So why can I remember it so vividly?

Because of *emotion*. Being told I looked beautiful on a day when I felt lost, confused, frustrated, and alone had far more impact than it would have on other days. It made me feel hopeful and reassured and had nothing to do with how I looked, but rather the wonderful feeling of being on the receiving end of kindness when I really needed it.

When you feel things, good or bad, they mean more to your brain, and so those stories stick.

A Significant Moment

This component will become even more important in the following chapter, but for now, as I tell all of my business storytelling clients, a great story is not a sprawling, epic phenomenon. Self-stories are little snapshots in time. They're significant for their impact, not their size. The compliment at the gas pump, the weigh-in at elementary school. Sitting across from an unhappy customer in a fluorescently lit boardroom. The elation of a spontaneous coffee shared with a friend because you both just happened to "have a minute." Compelling stories happen in little slices of time. Remember that.

Specific Details

Details are memorable. They make stories sticky and more believable. Marketers use them to make the stories of their products or services stick in your mind, and your brain does the same thing with far less effort. One of my favorite things is when someone shares a story they found and to hear in their voice the disbelief at how many minute, seemingly insignificant details they could recall—like remembering exactly where their car was parked in a story from ten years ago, while they couldn't remember where they parked at the mall the day before.

The value in understanding the components of what makes stories sticky is twofold. First of all, it's helpful to know why these particular icebergs form and hang around. It isn't necessarily because of their magnitude; sure, we remember the milestones, the big happenings in our lives, but these components explain why moments our conscious brain has deemed insignificant haven't melted away. Second, knowing how to make a story sticky is critical when you begin to choose the stories that *do* serve you in the next chapter— you want those new stories to hang around and form new icebergs of their own; the stickier, the better.

ACKNOWLEDGE THE DRAGONS

On December 11, 2002, then psychologist and now bestselling author and thought leader Jordan Peterson gave a presentation to a group of alumni of the University of Toronto. As part of the lecture, he read them a children's book intended for four-year-olds called *There's No Such Thing as a Dragon* by Jack Kent.

In the story, a little boy tells his mother there is a dragon in the house. The mother replies that dragons aren't real and continues about her day, as does the boy—and as does the dragon, who grows larger. As the day continues, both the mother's denial and the dragon grow until the big green beast carries the family's home down the street on its back. Only when the young boy finally asserts that the dragon is real and pets it on the head does the dragon shrink enough to crawl onto the mother's lap. "Why did it grow so big?" the mother asks. "I'm not sure," says the boy. "I think it just wanted to be noticed."

This was where participants in my group found themselves. Like the dragon, their stories grew over time, taking up more space. After participants felt the initial shock of how readily and vividly negative stories existed in their subconscious, the next realization was just how long their stories had been running amok in their lives. In many cases, it was *decades*.

The collective strength of these stories dictates the path our lives take, robs us of joy, and keeps us playing small—all while they stay almost completely under the radar, leaving us to wonder: *How did I end up here? Why can't I seem to break through and get over there? And what can I do about it?*

It all starts with seeing the stories for what they really are; to break the mass apart, analyze what has compressed together to keep you frozen in place.

Get out your icepicks; we're going on an excavation mission.

Your Mission, If You Choose to Accept It

One important thing to note: this excavation is not so that you can dwell or ruminate on the negative experiences in your life. It is intended to raise your awareness and bring to light the stories that are on repeat and influencing your actions. We're not looking to give these stories power but rather to see they already have it. And *not* addressing them only makes the problem worse. Nor is it about *erasing* bad stories. So far, there's no magic pill for highlighting a block of memory like text on a screen and erasing it.

No, we can't erase bad stories. And we don't want to give them more power than they already have. What we *can* do, as with dragons, is acknowledge their presence, then get to know them a little better before turning our attention to stories that serve us better.

As Peterson said, "If your path from point A to B is being blocked by something that you're afraid of, you better learn to confront it, because if you don't, it will grow and expand until it turns into the kind of dragon that occupies your whole house."

It's certainly easy to behave like the mother in the story—to ignore the stories, to pretend that, since you can't really see them, they're not really there. And while I don't believe our negative self-stories are eager to be in the light—I am pretty sure they are most comfortable in the shadows—ignoring them means they will eventually crowd out the good that is possible.

ANALYZING YOUR ICEBERGS

With that in mind, the first step in the analysis is to get a sense of the stories. The full, sticky stories that make up your iceberg. Once you have caught your limiting story in action via an "I am" statement or one of the other clues, it's time to take a walk down memory lane. Ask yourself if there are particular moments in your past that, like individual story snowflakes, have melded together to form this glacier. In some instances, you'll be able to identify them right away; others might be a little more elusive. In that case, let me suggest a strategy I also mentioned in *Stories That Stick*: that our stories can be accessed through the *nouns* in our lives—the people, places, things, events.

Think about the important people in your life: relatives, colleagues, friends, coaches. Also think about the people who maybe weren't beacons of light, but actually had a negative impact on you: ex-partners, old bosses, estranged friendships. What specific memories do you have of them? Are there stories that happened that you're still holding on to? Think back to the important places in your life: the home you grew up in, the camp you went to each summer, your church, the office where you went to your first real job. As you think of each of those places, it's likely old stories will come back to you and that some of them might not be the greatest. Think back to important events in your life (a move, a promotion, a job loss, a wedding, a funeral) or times in your life (youth, teenage years, early adulthood, that year you lived in Asia)—there are stories there, too. Good stories, yes. But also stories that may be working against you.

There are very few rules here. You can go back to your earliest memories or as recent as last Tuesday. The story can be big or small. There can be many, or just one that is strong enough to take you down. The key is pushing past the iceberg statement itself and finding the rest of the stories that are propping it up. Once you find a few of these stories, at minimum, make a mental note of them. I would encourage you to jot them down somewhere or tell them, in shock and perhaps even amazement, to someone you trust: "You won't believe the story I remembered from my very first job that I think I've been holding onto without realizing it." You can even tell me. Send me a direct message on Instagram (@kindrahall) and tell me the stories you can't believe you remember. Again, we're not doing this to *reinforce* the trauma but rather *release* it. In fact, much like with dragons, research indicates that in dealing with anxiety and PTSD, one of the best approaches is reliving the experience to its fullest. Or in the words of one of my favorite storytellers, Kevin Kling: "By telling the story, it no longer controls me."

One rule I *do* have is *do not judge*. Do *not* say, "Well, that was so long ago it hardly matters anymore." Clearly, it does. If your subconscious is holding on to it, it matters. Do not say to yourself, "But that was such a small thing; it doesn't count." As they say in the theater: there are no small parts, only small actors. The same is true for your stories. It's not the size of the story but rather the *emotion* behind it. And as discussed in part I, because our negative emotions like fear, shame, sadness, or regret come with an evolutionary boost, even the smallest story sticks with us.

This is a judgment-free zone. If you discover a story in the iceberg, it counts.

THE SIX QUESTIONS

Once you have a story (or a handful of them) squirming in the flashlight of your consciousness, it's time to get to know it better. Here are the six key questions to ask yourself to better understand the stories that are holding you back.

Question #1: Where did this story come from?

Icebergs don't just appear from nowhere, and neither do stories. Some stories come from actual personal experience—things that happened to you, events that occurred, things you witnessed. These are the most prevalent stories—as the famous lyric from the Broadway sensation *RENT* goes, we have 525,600 minutes each year, and each one of them has the possibility of becoming a story. Depending on how long you've been around, that's a lot of content.

In addition to *those* stories, there is another set: those that are handed down or handed over from friends or family members. Sometimes these stories are shared with us against our will—if you've ever sat at the adult table during a holiday gathering and endured Aunt Susan's story about being rejected by her first-pick college or Uncle Frank's failed attempt at a real estate empire, you know what I'm talking about. (Which begs the question, why do we long to leave the kids' table? Stay as long as you can!)

There is mounting evidence that the elements of stories—emotions, or rich sensory detail—can be handed down through generations, not just orally or through old journal entries but through our actual DNA.[1]

And then there are stories in that big, icy mass that we actively seek. Anytime we're trying to make sense of a situation or make a decision or get advice, what we often receive are stories. This makes sense, of course, because humans are storytelling creatures. So it's only logical that when asked for perspective from a friend, we'd offer a story in response. And *because* they are stories, they stick with us.

The Baby Weight Wait

I was about six months pregnant with my first child, and, ever the overachiever, I had managed to put on roughly double the amount of weight recommended for the *entirety* of a pregnancy. And while my doctor didn't seem overly concerned, I was starting to get nervous. How on earth was I going to get all this weight off once the baby was born? I decided to ask one of my friends who had recently had a baby—certainly she would have some advice.

I'll never forget where I was when I spoke with her. I was on the phone, sitting in my car at the gas station (strange, why do so many of my stories seem to happen at gas stations?) waiting for the pump to fill the tank, and my dear friend told me the story of herself and many of her friends who kept about ten pounds per kid. "It's just what happens," she said, matter-of-factly, and then went on to tell me more about how busy life gets, all the responsibility, the limited amount of time for yourself, etc., etc., etc. I remember hanging up the phone and staring blankly out the windshield as the story sank in. *Ten pounds per kid?* I had asked for a story. Ask and you shall receive. (I'll share how this story ended in the next chapter.)

Regardless of *where* the story comes from, stories are what they are. They come from whence they came. You can't change their origin. But understanding those origins is an important step in choosing a better story. Asking, "Where does this story come from?" creates the opportunity to actively *accept* versus passively *adopt* the stories that cross our paths.

RELATED QUESTIONS

- What is my earliest memory that relates to this story?
- Can I track this story over time?
- How have I expanded or built on this story since it began?

Question #2: Is this story true?

Lori Gottlieb, author of the runaway bestseller *Maybe You Should Talk to Someone,* has said that "as humans, we are all unreliable narrators. We think we are telling the accurate version of the story, but of course, what we're telling is a story through our subjective lens."[2] That subjectivity alone is cause for us to stop and take a closer look. Yes, inner stories are sometimes straightforwardly true. Sometimes, a story's truth changes with the passage of time. At other times, a story is true from one perspective, but if you turn it slightly to catch it from a different angle, its truth shifts in a way that doesn't make it false but adds dimension.

The malleability, the amorphousness, of a story is one of its most beautiful attributes. However, because of our desire for things to be black and white, set in stone, right or wrong, we miss the greatest gift a story has to give, and that is to change as we do.

Newlywed Bliss?

When I was a newlywed, I was struggling to adjust to merging my life with a man who, although he was wonderful, was also totally oblivious about what it meant to live with a woman. On the day I moved into the condo we would call Our Home, I was trying to figure out where all my belongings would reside. Michael told me he had it all figured out and pointed toward the maroon ottoman that matched the maroon couch he had purchased at Costco and matched the wall he had also painted, of all colors, maroon.

The ottoman. That is where my things would go. In a pile on the ottoman.

He noticed my eyes widen when he suggested it (you gotta give him credit for that), and so he offered that the rest of my things could go down in his storage locker in the parking garage. Like, if my mascara rolled off the top of the pile of my belongings on the ottoman, I could move it to the storage locker and just put my makeup on down there.

Michael's unique lot in life, however, is that he married a professional storyteller. It is literally my *job* to take experiences from my life, many of which would now involve him, and pass them on to the world as stories. Sometimes in books. Sometimes on social media. And, as was the case in this instance, sometimes at live events.

One night I was invited to tell stories at a late-night storytelling show. There I told a story that was about the rules I had set for myself when it came to life and men—and it was composed of a series of mini-stories, like the ottoman story, that were all about Michael and his silly, oblivious ways that had broken all of my rules. It was funny, it was a little racy, it was endearing, and it was told through the unmistakable lens of a newlywed, a young woman who still had stars in her eyes, whose relationship had not been tested by children or lack thereof, by job loss or business failure, by big decisions or the weight of decades of small ones.

After I finished telling my story, the crowd in the tiny black box theater applauded, but the only hand-clapping that mattered to me was from one man. No. Not Michael. He wasn't there. He was at a water polo tournament. Rather, my mentor and legendary storyteller Donald Davis. He approached me after the event, congratulated me on my storytelling, and said one of the most important things I would ever hear. "I loved your stories. I loved them. And I can't wait to hear what these stories will sound like in five years or ten years." His eyes twinkled. "That's what stories do," he said. "They change."

I believed him then, and I understand it more now. What I loved about Michael would morph and expand when I watched him hold his son for the first time. The story about the ottoman would mean something different after ten years of marriage and moving our family from sprawling suburban bliss to an apartment in Manhattan and surviving a pandemic. Even the definition of a broken rule would change as we wrote and rewrote our rules together.

Of course, as a professional storyteller, I *have to* go back and revisit old stories to see how the lens of time changes them; otherwise, I run out of material. But as an everyday human who isn't prepping for stage time at a storytelling festival, we don't have the same overt motivation to ask this question.

Each story for each person will have different considerations when it comes to truth—the iterations are endless. The most important thing, then, is to start with the question: Is this story true?

RELATED QUESTIONS

- Was it *ever* true?
- Was it true at one point, but now, with the gift of time and experience, the truth has shifted?
- Was it true for *me* and not just for the person who told it to me?

Question #3: Why is the story there?

There are no pointless stories.

If you uncover a story in your iceberg, it is there for a reason. *Understanding* that reason is an important piece of this journey.

Maybe the story was there to keep you safe, but the danger is no longer there. Maybe it was there to keep you humble, but now it's more important for you to be bold. Maybe the story is there because someone who mattered to you told it to you, and stories from people we trust have more sticking power than stories from people we're indifferent to; but even so, the story is no longer relevant. Did the story arrive at a time when you were healing from something, and help you get to the other side but now is keeping you there and holding you back, like excess scar tissue that builds up and, overstaying its welcome, causes other issues?

This question is about acknowledging that every story has some value and, as a result, realizing that you don't need to be ashamed of yours. You weren't ashamed of the crib you outgrew as a child; it's a natural part of growing up. But imagine if your parents put you in a crib as a baby to keep you safe and then never transitioned you out. You spent the night after prom in your crib.

You took your crib with you to college, moved it into your first home. That would be ridiculous, and yet, when it comes to our stories, this is common. And extremely problematic.

Fortunately, you're here. You know what to do, and you're already in the process of doing it.

Asking "Why is the story there?" allows you to eliminate shame, see the story for what it is, and release it.

RELATED QUESTIONS

- How does this story keep me where I am?
- How is it protecting me?
- What am I afraid of?

Question #4: What price do I pay for this story?

In 1989, the biggest earthquake in nearly a century struck San Francisco, killing sixty-three people, injuring nearly four thousand, and causing some six billion dollars in property damage.

I was a kid living in Minnesota at the time. The earthquake would have had little to do with me, except that on that day my dad was in San Francisco for business. I still remember my mother screaming into the kitchen phone tethered to the wall as she tried to figure out exactly what was happening and whether my father was okay. He was fine but came home with stories of sidewalks rolling and pieces of the hotel wall in his suitcase.

I thought it was cool; my mother did not. She decided right then and there that she would never, ever go to California. *Ever.*

That story kept her east of the Mississippi for a very long time. And then I moved to Arizona, where I met a man from San Diego, and we decided to have our wedding in, you guessed it, California.

My mother was at a self-storytelling crossroads. She could continue to tell herself the very true and terrifying story from twenty years earlier and let it dictate her actions, but that would mean not attending her daughter's wedding. The choice was obvious, and she and my father sat proudly in the front row the day I married the love of my life, but I'm certain the decision didn't come without some consideration.

Fair warning: your stories aren't always going to be as obvious, and the price isn't always going to be as clear-cut as missing your daughter's wedding, but know that the stories you tell yourself always come at a price. The price is happiness. The price is self-actualization. The price is health. The price tags are as varied and limitless as each individual human desire—but a negative self-story always costs something.

When it comes to the stories we tell ourselves, there are no free rides. What do you give up each time this story scurries around in your subconscious? Stories that serve the status quo work in direct opposition to stories that help you cross the gap in your life. What price are you paying for them?

RELATED QUESTIONS

- What would my life be like if this story were gone?
- What am I missing out on because of this story?
- How do I behave when this story is in play?

Question #5: Does this story serve me?

Meet Seema Bansal.

When Seema Bansal received flowers on Valentine's Day, she wasn't quite sure what to think.

If her new boyfriend was trying to impress her, it wasn't working. The flowers were terrible. They were nearly dead and lay limply in an ugly plain box.

Still, it seemed wrong not to acknowledge them. But Seema was in Vancouver, and her boyfriend, Sunny, was in New York, so she sent him a photo of the flowers and thanked him.

He was mortified. The flowers he'd ordered were most definitely *not* the ones she'd received. The whole situation quickly became a joke between them.

But then the joke changed. Seema, the daughter of immigrant parents, had grown up watching her father's entrepreneurial struggles. *We can do this better,* she thought.

Sunny agreed. Their conversations continued, and what started as a joke turned into a business idea. Before long, Seema was planning to invest her savings in a brand-new venture with her brand-new boyfriend and move from Vancouver to New York.

Not everyone was thrilled.

"There were so many naysayers," she recalled. "It started with my parents. They were just trying to be supportive, but they were scared that I was moving and using my life savings to start a business. I had a lot of friends in my ear saying this wasn't a smart decision. It was discouraging. I had a really hard time kind of figuring out who was in my corner."

The unexpected response to Seema's plans was a blow. And it brought old stories to life.

Seema's father had immigrated to Canada with almost nothing, then worked as a laborer, until he took a chance and secured a large loan from friends and family to start his own business. It was an enormous risk at the time, and it paid off.

On the surface, it seemed like that story should only encourage Seema to leap with both feet into her new venture. But stories are tricky. When Seema's father was cautious rather than supportive, a different story emerged. One that she shared in common with Sunny, who came from a similar background.

What was she thinking? Their parents had sacrificed to make sure their families would be okay. Was Seema going to risk all that? Her father's uncertainty about the business venture only added to her worries. Were she and Sunny disrespecting everything their parents had done for them on a whim?

"We couldn't make a mistake," Seema said. While it wasn't their parents' money on the line, it was their sacrifices.

Before long, Seema's story of new relationships and new opportunities had become, "You shouldn't move to a different country with a guy you just met to start a new business."

One of the most important questions you'll ask of the stories you find is: *Does this serve me?*

It is the most personal. It is the one only *you* can answer.

It is also the most difficult.

Because chances are, if you're asking it in the first place, the answer is probably *no*. No, the story is *not* serving you. And that means you have some work to do.

For Seema, that work wasn't easy. Reconciling what your gut is telling you about a new business and relationship with the competing stories of the people who even made dreaming possible for you is not for the faint of heart. And though her father gave her his blessing at the airport just as she was leaving Vancouver for New York City, the story followed Seema through many late nights when the business was struggling.

At first, they were running the business out of a one-bedroom apartment, Seema making the floral arrangements, and her boyfriend doing the deliveries, sometimes as far away as Connecticut or Maryland. As they struggled to figure out how to scale the business, Seema faced her old story time and time again.

"I would go to sleep crying every night. I would cry, but I would always be like, okay, but it's going to work. It's gonna work. It's gonna happen."

And happen it did.

Seema and Sunny's flower business, Venus ET Fleur, has gone from tiny start-up to globally known luxury brand. They ship worldwide, have swanky retail boutiques in London and New York, and have been lauded by celebrities like Oprah and the

Kardashians. But the only path to doing it meant letting go of old stories.

Only you can decide if a story serves you. And be aware that your answer might go against everything you thought you knew or believed. If you were raised in a family of doctors and have a sub-conscious library full of stories that end with, "and then I became a doctor and lived happily ever after," but putting a stethoscope around your neck feels more like a hundred-pound weight than a calling, it might be time to revisit those stories.

As Seema told me, "The thing that I learned from that entire experience is I just have to trust my gut and believe in myself. You have to trust your journey and keep going."

Question #6: Where am I in this story?

This is my favorite question and the one that alone has the power to change your life.

Miss Americana

I don't remember what day it was or when we watched it, but I'll never forget one moment in the documentary *Miss Americana* about the transcendent pop star Taylor Swift. In the scene, it is Grammy nomination day 2018 and Taylor is on the phone with an unnamed woman. The woman tells Taylor that, while she is still waiting on the full list of nominees, at that moment, in the main categories, Taylor's album *Reputation* was not nominated.

We've all felt our own version of disappointment. When the game-winning shot hits the rim. When, despite the final-hour push, the sales quota goes unreached. When we were hoping to get a really big yes, and got a really heartbreaking no. We've all been in that moment when something we worked really hard on, or something we thought was one thing turns out to be something else, namely failure . . . that moment when, for a second, we slip into that strange space where time stands still and speeds up all at the same time. It is in that slice in time where our subconscious takes us on a wild ride, flashing our entire catalog of stories before our eyes and begging us to reach the conclusion that "This story is over. I am a failure." Because if *that* is our conclusion, we'll stop and stick to safer pastures.

The documentary footage captures Swift at this exact crossroads and, for Taylor, it's a hugely weighted moment. "My entire moral code as a kid and now is a need to be thought of as good," she says. "I'd been trained to be happy when you get a lot of praise . . . those pats on the head were all I lived for."

Then we see the gifts of a master self-storyteller at work.

Taylor takes a breath, pauses for just a second, and then she says, both aloud and to herself: "This is good . . . this is fine . . . I just need to make a better record."

There was something about the way in which she said it— like it wasn't about being better according to someone else, but better according to *her*. And with that simple statement, Swift accesses what is perhaps the most important piece of the self-storytelling process. She decides this is not the end of her story; it's the *middle*.

A story can be created in an instant, and yet, miraculously, a story is also simultaneously as long and perpetually unfolding as life itself. An end can be a beginning; a beginning can be a middle. The middle of one story can be the end of another. When it comes to our self-stories, there are endless possibilities and possible combinations, but our default mode is to see stories as *finished*—as completed things that are true, permanent states of being. We like to put a period in the end, a title at the beginning, and go from there.

Taylor could have easily put a period at the end of that story and called it done. *I have already achieved all the success that was meant for me. I've already summited; this is the slow slide down the backside of the music industry mountain. The End.* Instead, profoundly aware that when it comes to her story, the pen is exclusively hers to hold, she deems this the middle of the story.

You can do the same. If you don't like the way the story ended, don't end the story there.

Make it the middle.

And here's the thing you should know about middles: Middles are *messy*. Middles are hard. It's confusing and full of conflict. It can feel unfair. You might feel frustrated or wronged and be fully justified in both. But that's just how middles are. And in recognizing that, in trusting it, you free yourself just a little bit. Eventually, over time, the story plays out. In hindsight, the events will no longer be random acts of devastation but stepping-stones that either brought you closer to your goals or taught you lessons you needed to learn until you reached an ending you're satisfied with.

You might, for example, have a money story that comes from a childhood, or even generations of childhoods, wrought with the pangs of poverty. And you might be living that story right now, struggling with a low income, or deeply in debt, or fearful of making a financial leap. But that doesn't mean the story is *over*. You're not at the end; you're in the middle.

Asking *where am I?* isn't about trying to predict the end of the story. It's simply about acknowledging that *the story isn't over*. And that decision is entirely yours. *You* get to decide. If you don't like the way a story ends, *then don't end it*.

Imagine if every negative story that is holding you back, through the process of this analysis, became the middle of your great story.

When you start looking below the surface of the water at the enormous mass of stories you've collected over your lifetime, your excavation will reveal stories with periods at the end—periods that act as great steel weights tied around the ankles of your self-belief and that pull you into the depths. When you find these stories, I challenge you to ask, *Where am I in this story?* Take out your red pen and mentally transform every period into a comma, a *pause*, while you wait to see how the rest could unfold.

RELATED QUESTIONS

- Why do I think this story is permanent?
- What could happen that would send the story in a new direction?

THE FREEDOM TO CHOOSE

Once you catch a story at work, a handful of questions is all it takes to go beneath the surface and see what's really there. You'll be able to spot the signs of a story at work, to identify its triggers, and to see its impact on your life. You'll take the invisible and make it *visible*.

And then? Well, that's when the fun really begins.

Because once you've begun to better understand the stories that run wild below the surface of your consciousness, you're in a position to *change* them. To tell a different story.

Make no mistake, the better stories are there.

You just have to *choose* them.

Exactly how to do that is what we'll talk about next.

CHOOSE

Reauthor a New Story that Serves You

Great stories happen to people who can tell them.

—IRA GLASS

I was on a call with my editor discussing cover options for this book.

At that point, he hadn't read a single word, but like the rest of us, he was excited about the impact it might have. What he didn't know was that the call wasn't all sunshine and rainbows for me.

I was sharing a few of my ideas for book covers, one of which included the image of someone standing on the tip of an iceberg looking down into the water where the rest of the mass lurked below the surface.

"Yeah," he said. "I don't think I like the iceberg image. It just seems so ominous, you know? Too big. Too arduous."

Uh-oh.

I tried to hide the panic that was rising in my chest. As of that moment, I had two entire chapters dedicated to the icebergs within us and here my editor was shooting it down for being too heavy.

Here's why you're still reading about icebergs, despite my editor's concerns: icebergs *are* heavy. They are beyond heavy. They are ominous. They are big and intimidating. They are everything he said they were. Which is why it is so important to embrace them.

To see the icebergs and understand them and, in the process, *own* them.

That's exactly what you've done so far. You've learned to:

- Make the invisible *visible* by catching a glimpse of those icebergs that your inner storyteller is shoving into the sea in front of you.
- Look beneath the glassy surface and see the many stories hiding there for what they really are.

My editor is right: taking a good look at what's really happening in our minds when we're not looking can be a big, scary task.

And while, yes, there are stories in your life's iceberg that are holding you back, and they are indeed ominous, there are so many *more* stories that are good!

There are stories of triumph. Stories of love and friendship. Stories of alignment and courage and joy. No matter who you are or where you come from or how you were (or were not) raised, good stories have occurred. You've been kind and experienced kindness. You've faced fear and persevered. You've done hard things and are better for them. Even if they feel too small or too few to matter, the positive stories are *there* and they can serve you so much better.

Much like our negative stories, these positive stories can be big and expansive, or they can be as small and fleeting as a compliment on a tough day. But more importantly, if it were possible to take an accurate inventory, more often than not, the *good* stories would far outnumber the bad ones. Of course, with our negativity bias humming away, giving preferential treatment to the scary, painful stories as a means for survival, you might never guess that was the case.

That's why this chapter is the most important of the entire book. Because although biology may be working against us, free will is still in your hands. You have the ability, the right, and, if the Emerald City is what you seek, the responsibility to *choose*.

Choose to tell yourself stories that *serve* you. Choose to *seek out* and then *amplify* the stories that get you across the gap. This chapter details five specific strategies for doing so.

If the yellow brick road is the path to where you want to go, then each individual slab of stone is a story you *choose* to tell yourself. Every time you encounter a limiting belief, or you are triggered by a post on social media, or fall off the healthy-eating wagon, or have another relationship fall apart, you're at a crossroads. You can allow your subconscious to run the show and chalk it up to the thing that "always" happens, *or* you can take control and use it as an opportunity to choose and tell yourself a better story.

TWO PITFALLS ON THE PATH TO BETTER STORIES

The first week of my one-on-one sessions with the participants was awesome. Everyone seemed readily able to *catch*; they came to their first meeting with a list of iceberg statements ready to share. They were also able to easily *analyze* where some of the statements might have come from. I found myself wondering if we would need four sessions; maybe it would only take two or three.

At the end of these first one-on-one sessions, each participant was to come back the following week with a couple of *positive* stories related to their limiting beliefs that they could *choose* to tell themselves instead.

The first session of the second week also started off great. The participant had no problem identifying some not-so-good stories that were playing on automatic repeat and keeping him second-guessing himself.

"Great," I said. "What stories did you find that you could choose instead?"

"Uh. Well. I know I'm good at my job. Let's see . . . I know that I am smart and a good leader?"

And that was pretty much the response from every single person. A few half-hearted sentences that sounded like they were pulled from a generic greeting card you buy at the drugstore check-out line.

I'll admit, I was a slight shade of concerned by this. But then I had an epiphany. What the participants were struggling with was exactly what businesses struggle with when they try to find their stories. Instead of finding actual moments and including the things that make stories sticky—the components we discussed in chapter 5, like emotions and details and characters—they shared generalizations, bullet points, and high-level empty talk or logic.

In business, this leads to bad sales pitches and failed marketing campaigns. But in *life*, it leaves you unarmed and unprepared for the battle to take back control of your subconscious.

With that new perspective, I was able to guide participants to find their stories by first sharing the key pitfalls of story-seekers and then teaching them the specific strategies for choosing stories to serve them better.

Pitfall 1: Choosing things that aren't stories

Meet Megan Tamte.

Megan is the cofounder of a thriving women's fashion concept called Evereve. In an era where the headlines say brick and mortar retail is dead, and despite a crippling pandemic, Evereve has defied logic by expanding their brand to stores from coast to coast—and doing it with zero debt.

When doubts set in or things get tough for Megan, which they inevitably do for all of us, she could look at the long list of retail shops across the country to reassure herself. She could turn to her financial statements to shore up her self-esteem. She could look in the mirror and say, "Megan, you got this."

But those things do very little to settle unease because *they're not stories*.

Generalizations aren't stories. Neither are statements. The goals you set for this year? They aren't stories either—they're just places you're aiming for. "I'm going to Italy" isn't a story. "I'm going to exercise more" isn't a story. Goals, aspirations, hopes, and dreams are wonderful things—but they aren't stories.

Instead, Megan has a set of *real* stories she can tell herself. Like the time, many years earlier, when she decided to get a part-time job at Crate & Barrel. She was a new mom and felt like she had lost a part of herself in the process. The job was fine, even if Megan's friends were questioning why she would give up her Tuesday and Thursday evenings and Saturday afternoons to work part-time at Crate & Barrel. It was nothing special, but it filled a hole that Megan was feeling at the time.

That in itself isn't the kind of story that would comfort Megan when she's feeling uneasy. But ten years into the start of Evereve, Megan and her cofounder husband decided to take on investors and sell part of the company. One of the very first people to come on board was none other than the cofounder and co-CEO of, you may have guessed it, Crate & Barrel.

When Megan told me the story of walking through the big glass doors of her former part-time job with the founder of Crate & Barrel, who was now her new investor, it was clear that moment meant more than any accolades, awards, or other non-story ever could.

Staring into the mirror before a meeting and saying, "I deserve this," is self-talk.

Staring into the mirror and reflecting, in detail, on the collection of moments and decisions and challenges and risks that led you to this point is self-*story*.

One has the elements of a great story; the other is a sentence. It's bravado. It's an affirmation. And those things are fine—but they aren't effective stories. When you look for better stories to tell yourself, make sure they are actual *stories* and not just lists of reasons. If change is what you're seeking, actual stories are what you need. Do they include the components? Can you see it replay in your mind like a movie?

If logic were effective, you wouldn't be here right now. What you need is a story.

Pitfall 2: Discounting small stories

Meet Erin.

A decade ago, Erin worked selling ad space for a local radio station. Now she owns her own thriving digital marketing agency. But despite her success, something was holding her back. She played it safe. She discounted her services when she shouldn't have. She took on clients she knew were a bad fit, all because she wasn't valuing herself or her skill.

There was something about Erin I really connected with—I felt that she and I were at similar crossroads. That what we thought *should* motivate us didn't, and what others thought was success didn't quite sit right. When Erin went looking for her stories, she mentioned her sprawling office and the team she employs. She mentioned her satisfied clients and her track record, all of which should make her feel pretty dang good about herself. And yet, even as she shared these things with me, they had that distinct flavor of, "I'm telling you what I think I'm supposed to be telling you."

I heard this a lot with my participants, and you'll likely struggle with the same thing. They wanted to find a story that was "good enough" by someone else's standards (in this case, mine) or that society would deem worthy. A story that was "big enough" to replace a lifetime of negative ones. This thinking is errant for several reasons.

First, while certainly there are likely big stories in your past of when things went wrong, there are also many more tiny negative stories, just like the ones in this book. If small negative stories can hold you back, then small positive stories can propel you forward.

Second, you don't need anyone to greenlight your stories. Not me, not Hollywood, not your sister-in-law. It really doesn't matter what anyone else thinks. If a story fires *you* up and gets *you* excited to skip down your yellow brick road, then go for it!

In Erin's case, there was this one moment at her old job selling radio ads, a story she shied away from at first because she thought it was too trivial or immaterial, but even I could tell as she retold it to me on a whim that the story really motivated her.

When Erin was twenty-four, she was crushing her work. As she said, "I was knocking goals out of the park." And so she bought herself a BMW. A fancy sports car.

There were a dozen more important things Erin could have done with that money. She could have invested it. There were college funds to build and a mortgage to pay for.

But she loved that car. Each time she sat in it was a confirmation of her success. And she'll never forget the first day pulling into the office parking lot in her new car and how she turned the heads of her colleagues. A few were a little snarky, a few nodded in congrats, but none of them, including Erin, could deny what it took to earn a car like that.

Eventually, her growing family made the car impractical, and Erin happily let it go. But now, at a time when she needs a success story to help her make the right decisions in her business, it's the memory of that car she's turning to.

Yes, a story about a car may seem trivial, but to Erin, it wasn't. It was an expression of her hard work and the joy it brought her, which is inherently valuable. It was small, but it was hers, and it worked.

You may be tempted to judge your stories. To quickly write off stories that seem "unworthy" or "too trivial" by some outside set of standards. Don't. If the story feels good to you, use it. If at some point you outgrow that story, that's okay too. It just means you need to find some new ones.

And how do you find those new ones? Exactly how do you go about parting the seas of your negative stories to find ones that work?

Let's find out.

FIVE WAYS TO CHOOSE A BETTER STORY

To choose is to gain control over your stories, and, in turn, your future. And though better stories may have eluded you until now, the following five options for choosing better ones will leave you with an endless supply of positive self-story options.

1. Replace: Out with the bad, in with the good

This is the most straightforward method for choosing a better story, and its premise is simple: once you identify a story that doesn't serve you, *look for another that proves that story wrong.* My research was filled with them this year:

- The woman who was convinced she'd never be consistent at exercise—she chose to tell herself the story of when she trained for and ran a half marathon.
- The man who believed he had to prove himself to be respected. He chose instead to tell himself stories of the many accolades, compliments, and letters of gratitude he'd received simply as a result of being himself.
- The woman who didn't think she had what it took to start her own business. She chose to tell herself the story of the time she studied and took one of the hardest tests in her field—and passed when no one thought she would.
- The man who berated himself for never being the top sales-man in his company. He chose to tell himself the story of what work is *really* about for him—his relationships and values—and decided to own the fact that his definition of success was slightly different than his colleagues. (Look forward to his story in the next chapter.)

2. Reinterpret: See another side of a self-story

I have always had extremely thick hair. It's not particularly unruly; there is just a lot of it. I am often asked by strangers on social media, friends who haven't seen me in a while, and even once by my nine-year-old son if I got hair extensions. Nope. It's just my hair.

Now, as an adult, I love my hair. And even as a kid, I loved it for the most part—except for that one time, right at the end of fourth grade when the movie *Hook* was a huge hit, and Julia Roberts had, as my mother claimed, "the cutest pixie haircut," and she took me into the salon and had my hair all chopped off and I had to explain to random people at restaurants and the grocery store that I was, indeed, a girl.

So there was that. And, the only other time I hated my hair was when my mother brushed it. I don't know what it was, but every time she put the brush to my hair, it felt like entering a torture chamber. She would brush, and I would flail my head backward and scream.

"I'm not even brushing hard!" she would say, barely keeping her cool, as I continued to flail and scream.

It was a constant battle and one I had all but forgotten—until I had to brush my *own* daughter's hair. I don't know what it is, but every time I put the brush to her hair, it feels like entering a torture chamber. I brush, and she flails her head backward and screams. "I'm not even brushing hard!" I say, barely keeping my cool. It's a constant battle that usually ends with me threatening to cut all her hair off—

Wait a minute.

I have told the story of my bad haircut hundreds of times as a short piece of an opening keynote story. I watch the audience nod in recognition—who hasn't endured a bad haircut (often inspired by their mother)? But it wasn't until just recently that I put two and two together. I didn't get all my hair chopped off because of Julia Roberts! My mother got my hair cut off so she wouldn't have to deal with brushing it anymore.

This isn't a life-changing story; it's a life-*illustrating* story. It shows the power we have to see, understand, and therefore *use* a story in a different way. If it's true of something as mundane as hair-brushing, what else might it be true of? That time at the family reunion that led to you never speaking to your brother again? The time at work that you didn't get the promotion? Stories, especially self-stories, are always up for interpretation. Like powerful books you've already read, sometimes returning to a story with more wisdom and experience reveals something that serves you.

3. Reroute: Use one story to inspire another

Meet Meredith.

Meredith works as an independent math consultant in New York City and, for ages, has wanted to start her own niche business serving parents and schools. And though she's more than qualified and has everything required to get it off the ground, something keeps stopping her. Every time she sets aside time to work on it, she ends up staring at a blank page or, at best, scribbling a few notes before getting up to tend to her daughters.

Finding the statements that are holding her back was easy for Meredith. "I'm a procrastinator." "I'm not successful out of my comfort zone." "I'm destined to always work for others." "I'm not intrinsically motivated."

But the trouble was when we moved to try to replace her old stories with better ones. Any offer of a new story to tell was quickly shot down.

Meredith has what I call a strong *editor*. When you try to do something you truly have never done before, your inner storyteller is likely to push back. This overactive "editor" is like something within you holding a red pen and striking down ideas or finding flaws before you even get a chance to fully explore them. As it was for Meredith, finding new stories to choose can be a struggle in these situations, because the editor throws them out the second they show themselves.

Perfectionists, Type As, Enneagram 1s—you know this editor well, but no one is immune to it. And even though the editor isn't lying per se—often the editor is pointing at real stories based on previous experience or lack thereof—the editor certainly isn't serving the goal of getting unstuck.

What gets the editor fired up the most is when you don't actually *have* any past experience. There's no directly related story that seems powerful enough to convince the editor. Often, we'll try to overcome the editor with enthusiasm, optimism, and self-talk. But just as often, we fall short. The red pen is often mightier than the affirmation sword.

This is where rerouting comes in. It's not about lying to the overactive editor; it's about outsmarting it. It's about finding a story from another area of life in which you successfully applied principles that you can reapply to your new aspiration.

Meredith desperately wanted to get past her editor (and after hearing her idea, I sincerely hope she does—it's genius). And for a while, I almost wondered if this strategy wouldn't work for her. But then she finally found a story, buried more than fifteen years earlier when she moved to New York City.

It was 2005, and Meredith had moved to the city with her then-boyfriend. Her first year wasn't easy.

"I remember I was by myself for the first two or three weeks," she said, "and realizing how you can be in a city of eight million people and feel completely alone . . . then I had a super hard year teaching that year."

It was hard, but it also wasn't impossible. Meredith felt she'd made progress with the students and built rapport, and, despite almost-daily tests of her limits at the beginning of the year, by the end of the year she was proud of what they had accomplished together.

Still, change kept coming. Her boyfriend wanted to leave New York, and Meredith agreed. But after a terrible winter, they broke up. That summer, Meredith headed back to the city.

"Through Craigslist, I found random people to live with who weren't serial killers, magically. Then I moved through a series of apartments and jobs and I have been here ever since."

When I asked Meredith to put that story up against the ice-berg statements from earlier, the light bulb came on. How does someone who "isn't successful out of her comfort zone" or "not intrinsically motivated" pick up and move not once but twice to one of the most challenging cities on earth to live with strangers?

Meredith was not the person her stories were telling her she was. And now, she could face down the editor by rerouting to a story that proved she *did* have the essential ingredients to strike out on her own.

Rerouting helps pull stories from one area of life to support the growth of another. The key to this approach is to think about the bigger themes involved. Imagine you're applying for a sales posi-tion, for example. You think you'd be good at it, but every time you start prepping for the interview, the editor shoots down anything you say because you've never actually been in sales. Well, what does a successful career in sales require? Being able to get people to see the value in what you have to offer and to say yes. Are there stories you can reroute to that fit those themes? Maybe you raised funds for a community garden a few years back or helped your daughter sell Girl Scout cookies.

Sales also requires being able to handle rejection. Maybe you were initially turned down by your top college but were able to write a response that reversed their decision.

Sales requires motivation and hunger. Maybe you were always the first one on the field for soccer practice and the last one to leave and helped your team win a championship.

These themes are directly related to the *job,* even if you've never done sales, and can help drown out the editor.

4. Research: Borrow a story from someone else

Many of our default stories aren't actually our own, but rather stories we adopted from others in our life. Those stories may be largely unconscious, but it *is* possible to *intentionally* use someone else's story to serve you.

You remember, from the previous chapter, the story my friend told me about baby weight? About how you gain and keep ten pounds per kid? I remember trying that story on for a minute to consider what my life would be like if that were the case and if I liked that story for myself.

It turns out I didn't. And so I went "researching" for a better one.

The first place I looked was my spin studio, where many of my friends were both mothers and in amazing shape. I asked for their stories, and they told me about the transition back to exercise, finding the time, the challenge of prioritizing yourself. They told me funny stories and stories that made me tired just listening to them. "It might take some time," they told me. "But you'll be back and better than ever."

I decided I liked those stories better, so I borrowed them. And they became the stories I told myself as I gained seventy-five pounds and, after having my son, lost eighty. I felt the strongest of my life after having each of my children, and I fully believe it was because of the story I was gifted by my friends that then became the story I chose to tell myself.

The dark side of borrowed stories

A warning: there is a danger with this approach.

Because we have access to so many stories via social media, and because some people appear to be *so* open about their story, it's easy to watch someone we think we know and to choose to tell ourselves *their* story as a means for choosing our own desired success—only to discover what they are sharing outwardly is not the whole story.

For example, there was a period in my career where I was, on a weekly basis and in the most random ways, compared to Rachel

Hollis. We were both midthirties entrepreneur mothers working with their husbands. We spoke at the same conferences at the same time or in consecutive years. Colleagues would mention it, friends over coffee. One time, I was at Barnes & Noble with my son picking up an issue of *SUCCESS* magazine featuring an article of mine. Bubbling with excitement and so proud of his mother, my son told the cashier, "My mama's in that magazine."

The woman pointed to the cover. "That's you?!" she asked me.

"No," my son said. "No, that's Rachel Hollis. My mom is on the inside somewhere."

With so many similarities, and considering her meteoric rise, it seemed only natural to listen to Rachel's stories and adopt them as my own. The hustle. The nonstop. The bigger and better. Host huge live events? Maybe I should work toward that. Clothing line? I mean, maybe. A documentary playing in theaters across the country? Perhaps. A daily IG live. A wildly popular podcast. A huge new office and big team.

There was a lot to consider, and not all of it felt quite right for me. Don't get me wrong, I love a good hustle, but after trying that story on for a while, I felt like other areas of my life suffered too much. I changed tack, while secretly wondering if that meant I'd never be "as successful" as Rachel.

It was particularly shocking, then, when I read the post announcing the end of Rachel's marriage to Dave Hollis. Clearly, there were things happening behind the screens and scenes in their story to which the rest of the world was not privy. Keep that in mind as you research other people's stories to adopt and inspire your own. Unless they are someone you know, sometimes the whole story, including its price, isn't always shared up front.

The stories you borrow come with a warning: *stories online may be different than they appear.*

Borrowed stories also exist dangerously close to *comparison*. If you have something you're working toward in any area of life, all it takes is a slight look to the right or left at the office or a finger swipe on social media to see an unlimited supply of people who are already doing it and doing it way better than you.

Logically, you know you only see their highlight reel. Yet, it's easy to think those people simply have something you don't. More money, more time, less stress, more luck, better genes, better connections—to your inner storyteller, they simply seem special in a way you're not.

I love watching the people, the authors, the inspirations, the men, and especially the women who are ahead of me. I know I can learn from them and see their example as a gift. However, I can also fall into the comparison trap, thinking I'll never get there or that they have something special that isn't available to me. Your mother wasn't wrong when she said comparison is the thief of joy; she simply failed to mention that comparison is also a perfect opportunity to tell yourself a better story.

5. Rewrite: Find a story that doesn't exist—yet

It was summertime and, after a particularly indulgent first few weeks, I decided to embark on a new fitness program. This was especially bold considering our family was supposed to be on vacation. It was *extra* bold because I've started workout programs before; three-week programs, ninety-day challenges, thirty-day boot camps—you name it, I've tried it. And I almost always fail. I make it to day two, and then it all falls apart. I'm too sore, I don't have time—I use all the low-hanging excuses I can find to justify quitting.

(As you'll read in part III, health and fitness stories are the ones I end up working on most often.)

So there I was, doing Workout #1. I was sweating. I was struggling. And I was repeating to myself, "Here I go again. Workout #1, and I'm going to find a reason to quit after Workout #3. That's what I always do." Bicep curl—"I'm going to quit soon." Burpee-burpee—"Yeah, I'll never do *this* exercise again." With every move,

I was literally planning my failure. Every time I lifted a weight or did a jumping jack, that was the story I told myself. I was doing reps for my body, yes, but what I was *really* doing was strengthening a story that didn't serve me in any way.

So, what to do?

- *Replace* wasn't cutting it. I didn't *have* any stories of successfully finishing a workout program.
- *Reinterpret* didn't work. I didn't see another way to view my past failures in a way that served.
- *Reroute* was an option. I had lots of "stick with it" stories from my professional life. But they didn't translate well—all they did was make me want to work instead of work out, which was the problem in the first place!
- *Research* for stories with other people didn't seem to help in this case, either. They just made me crabby, not motivated.

Instead, I decided to *rewrite*. I would create a story from scratch. A story about a future *me*. A story that hadn't happened—*yet*.

I told myself this story: After the workout series was complete, and I made it all the way through, which I would, I would treat myself and go shopping. I told myself the story of the exact dressing room I would walk out of—it was in a little boutique with the cutest summer clothes. I imagined the exact mirror I would stand in front of and how every outfit would make me feel incredible.

Suddenly, the story wasn't one of dread and impending doom; it was inspiring, exciting, and worth working toward. The challenge and pain during workouts, the things that used to make me want to give up, transformed into physical expressions of getting closer to that story and fueled me. And with *that* story, I made it through the entire program without missing a day.

Sometimes we have to rewrite. We have to tell ourselves stories that haven't happened yet. But I feel it's only fair to warn you: these stories are harder. It's not hard to make a story up—that part is fun.

But it's hard to override a negative story with one that hasn't happened yet. Your inner storyteller will fight back, telling you your head is in the clouds, telling you you're not in touch with reality.

What to do? Luckily, there's a chapter for that and it's coming next.

Icebergs take time. The stories blocking your way have been growing for years. Sometimes for a lifetime. A new story, however, is a fragile thing. It's fresh. Your new story is David up against the Goliath of your established stories who is blocking your path to the Emerald City.

No matter what strategy you use to choose your new story, that story needs to get a foothold. It needs to be deliberately *installed* into your life so that when you hear the cry of "Ahoy! Iceberg!" you'll be ready.

INSTALL

Putting Your New Self-Story to Work

Hope is not just a feeling; like love, it is a practice. It is a verb.
It is action.

—R. O. KWON

The five minutes before any presentation are the worst.

Any keynote speaker, musician, or actor waiting in the wings before the curtains open—heck, any salesperson sitting in the lobby waiting for the executive assistant to say the words "So-and-so will see you now"—will tell you that the moments right before "showtime" are intense. Always. And while many people put the fear of public speaking above the fear of death, for me, it was particularly problematic.

Because public speaking was my job. And not a job that was forced upon me, but one that I chose for myself. A job I almost lost to fear.

First, it should be said that I love the stage. I love sharing and being with the audience. Even when the pandemic hit and many of my presentations were broadcast virtually, I loved the idea that people I couldn't see were learning about the power of their stories. Plus, I'm really good at it. I'm the daughter of rock-band parents (Remember? My dad, Mike, and my mom started a rock band); the stage feels like home. And after decades of dedication to the research and application of storytelling, I was more than qualified for the job.

So, I had ample logic to combat any stage nerves. But fear doesn't work that way. My ancient brain saw the stage as a threat, and my body responded accordingly.

Multiple times a month, I would find myself standing in front of hundreds, or thousands, or, in some cases, tens of thousands of people. The number didn't matter; my response was the same: in the hours leading up to every event, I was wracked with fear. And not just your typical butterflies-and-sweaty-palms stuff. This was jump-off-the-balcony-pull-the-fire-alarm-catch-a-flight-to-Mexico-and-never-come-back fear. I would pace the hotel room, then the ballroom, then backstage—all while a voice only I could hear shouted in my mental loudspeaker, "You don't belong here! You have nothing to offer! You aren't telling them anything they don't already know! *You've failed before and you'll do it again.*"

You would think, after several years and hundreds of repetitions, the anxiety would subside. But it didn't. It just got worse. And the more success I found, the harder it became to manage.

I tried everything. More sleep. Less sleep. Exercise. Sitting still. Less coffee. More coffee. Meditation. Positive affirmations. Fasting. If it was legal, I tried it. None of it worked.

Clearly, there was something much bigger at play here, and for a while, I wondered if I would ever get to the other side of it. And though, without fail, the anxiety would subside within seconds of stepping onstage, the hours upon hours (sometimes weeks depending on the event and what was at stake) of torture leading up to it made me question whether I needed to find a new career.

I *know*: I'm a keynote speaker who speaks about storytelling. And, yes, looking back, I'm a little ashamed at how long it took me to realize the solution was storytelling itself (though in my defense, at the time I was presenting mainly about storytelling as it pertains to sales, marketing, and leadership in business). But eventually, it was clear even to me: if I was going to overcome this completely irrational and thoroughly unjustified fear of the stage, stories were my only hope.

So I started telling them—to myself.

To ease my crippling fear, I began doing the very thing this book suggests. I told myself stories that served me. And in this case, the ones that worked best weren't the stories of a time when things went amazing, and everyone loved me. Those did nothing to calm my nerves. Instead, I told myself stories of when things went terribly awry, and I still crushed it.

Remember the time, I'd tell myself, *that you got the stomach flu in the wee morning hours before a huge ninety-minute keynote for that tech company? You were so sick the AV team put a bucket offstage for you and had strict instructions to cut the mic if you went anywhere close to it. The audience never had a clue, and the presentation was amazing!*

I told myself about the time I was speaking in the Bahamas in front of 1,500 people and, about two-thirds of the way through and right before I was going to play a video of one of my case studies, the power went out. Like, *all* of the power. No more stage lights. No PowerPoint. No video. No microphone. The ballroom was a few emergency generator watts away from pitch blackness. As the person on the stage, everyone was staring at me with that "What do we do now?!" look.

I called out to the team at the AV table to ask if it was an emergency and confirm we didn't need to evacuate. They gave me the all-clear sign. I then called to my audience, "If I speak at this volume, can you all hear me?" They shouted *yes!* "Should I keep going?!" They shouted *yes!* And so, I did. Just me, my ideas, and a roomful of people who wanted to hear them.

I remember signing into Twitter later that afternoon to see tweets from the audience, and one from a fellow keynote speaker who was there said something like: "I've been doing this a lot longer and can't say I would've handled it as well. #totalpro"

I told myself about the time I was speaking in California and was supposed to catch a flight to Columbus, Ohio, for a keynote the next day—normal stuff. But there were storms across the

Midwest, and my flight was canceled. I ended up taking a red-eye to Indianapolis, arriving at dawn, then riding three hours to Columbus, and taking a nap for an hour in my hotel room. Then I headed to the stadium, where I spoke to ten thousand people for an hour.

The stories went on, but you get the picture. And so did my subconscious. I could remember every detail, every emotion, every image from each of these events. I could tell you the people I met, the shoes I was wearing, and exactly how tired I felt. They were the kind of stories that stick, and I started telling them to myself.

Methodically.

I reserved ten minutes in the morning before each keynote, sat down in the hotel room desk chair, and told myself the stories. As I walked to the ballroom, I replayed those stories. Backstage, in those gut-wrenching moments right before they say your name, these were the stories I had on repeat.

At first, it was very intentional. As time went on, gradually, these stories became automated. It was as if my subconscious fell in line with what I knew, logically, was true—that I was very good at my job, and there was no reason to be so anxiety-ridden. But logic alone wasn't going to do the job, nor was casual consideration of my previous success. I needed *stories*, installed in their full story glory, to finally put an end to the crippling doubt.

The impact of this installation was no small thing. Prior to choosing and then installing better stories, there were moments where, as I mentioned earlier, I wondered if I should quit. The darkness of my fear wasn't worth the light of the stage. I was at the top of my game, making seven figures in my dream job, and I almost threw in the towel.

Thank goodness I didn't. I am here writing this today because of this final, critical step in the self-storytelling process: to intentionally, methodically install the stories that serve you until they become the default from which your subconscious operates.

This is the step where life truly changes.

THE HABIT OF STORIES

By now, you know the power of your inner storyteller. You know how to catch stories at work, drag them into the light, and analyze them. You know how to choose better ones, ones that serve you and can propel you forward.

But let me warn you, habits are hard to break. In fact, some people would say that we never truly eliminate a habit at a neurological level—we can only create new ones that overshadow the old. The former habits, like icebergs, still lurk.

It's why it's so easy for us to "fall off the wagon" when it comes to bad habits. We do *so well* on the latest diet, and then have a bad day and eat an entire box of cookies. It's because the connections in the brain that form the habit are still there, and it may not take much to light them up again. Like an overgrown path in the woods, all it takes is a weed whacker, and the neural thoroughfare is ready for rush hour.

Stories are similar. They share the same neurological base—they're just bundles of connections in the brain. And that means your *old* stories—the ones you may have been telling and retelling for years—are never that far away. They can decay with time, just like habits, but the most compelling of them retain their strength for many years.

Fortunately, new stories run on the same system, and you can build and reinforce them in the same way. You absolutely can install stories that serve.

NEW KID ON THE MENTAL BLOCK

New stories are like a new kid in class—at first, they don't get much attention.

No one remembers the new kid for those first few birthday parties. People don't think to ask them to hang out. New stories, like new kids, simply aren't top of mind.

Part of the solution to this problem is one of exposure. The new kid keeps showing up, keeps trying, keeps hanging around, and eventually, everything works out. Likewise, if you keep telling yourself a new story long enough, it begins to take hold.

But this isn't a passive job. I remember when my son was the new kid in his second-grade class. He didn't sit back and hope someone would talk to him; he actively tried to figure out their interests. He started a comic-book club. He got the kids in his class interested in coin collecting. He made up games on the playground that others would want to join. Not all his efforts paid off immediately, but by the time third grade rolled around, he wasn't the new kid anymore. He was part of the group. My son was able to break free of a title that might follow some people through high school and replace it with something else.

Getting your good stories to stick, to make them as automatic as the negative ones once were, isn't something you can just sit back and trust your subconscious to handle—at least not at first. Elevating those better stories and automating them doesn't just happen. Not without practice. That is what this chapter is about: systematically, intentionally installing these chosen stories as your inner-narrative default. It's the fourth and final step in the self-storytelling process.

INSTALLING BETTER STORIES IN YOUR LIFE

In the previous chapter, we talked about choosing better stories and that there are always good story options—we just have to *choose* them. And while the simple act of recognizing that our lives are filled with positive, empowering stories is an improvement on a state of complete oblivion, if you're looking to change your life, we need to shift from choosing a story to really *using* it. There are four strategies to successfully install your new, chosen stories:

1. **Write** the stories that serve you.

2. **Share** your stories aloud.
3. **Plan** for the tough moments.
4. **Start** each day with your stories.

Taken separately, each of these strategies will increase the power of your self-storytelling; used together, they'll make you unstoppable.

STRATEGY #1: WRITE THE STORIES THAT SERVE YOU

There was a collective groan on the group Zoom when I announced this strategy to the participants I was guiding through the self-storytelling process—which is saying something, considering they were all on mute.

Most participants weren't huge fans of journaling. There were a few who were downright angry, citing things like being left-handed (actually a viable complaint, I think), fingers that were too big, and handwriting that was so bad that the act of writing alone sent them into a story spiral of unworthiness.

Before I say what I'm about to say next, I want you to know: I was vehemently opposed to turning this into a "journaling book," a book where I either a) included exercises in relevant chapters for you to write your thoughts or b) created a journal that accompanied the book as, like, a "bonus."

As I said to Michael, "I feel like everyone is telling everyone to journal, and it's just annoying, and I don't want the aversion to putting pen to paper to be a deterrent. This works without a journal." And I meant it.

Greenlighting Journaling

But then I listened to an interview with Matthew McConaughey.[1]

McConaughey's book, *Greenlights,* had just been released to much-deserved fanfare. It's essentially a compilation of his journal entries over several decades of his life. While I can't remember if he ever explicitly stated, "Journaling is the key to my success," it was clear throughout the interview that the act of sitting down, putting pen to paper, and writing about his life so that he could revisit those writings when he needed guidance or insight was an essential piece of his all-encompassing success (even aside from the fact that he turned those journals into a *New York Times* bestseller for many, many weeks).

It isn't just a McConaughey hunch that journaling is a valuable endeavor. Research shows that the act of writing does more than just help you remember. In general, writing things down is good for you. Writing helps you focus and acts as a mood booster, helping with depression and anxiety.[2]

More specifically to self-storytelling, the act of handwriting slows us down and forces us to think more thoroughly, process our thoughts more completely, and in our case, see the story a little more clearly. That, in turn, helps us recall what we write more easily later on.[3]

McConaughey believes there's the natural instinct to journal when things aren't going well; the act of writing helps us work through and make sense of the chaos. When I think back to the volumes of journals I wrote in my teen years and how I pretty much stopped as soon as the hormonal drama of my youth subsided, his belief resonated with me. But McConaughey's true secret is to do the opposite—to journal when things are going *well*. Write down when you are your happiest. Document your wins. Tell the *good* stories.

The push to journal when we feel down, while not inherently bad, is also an expression of our negative bias—we're focusing on the bad and forget the good. Instead, by documenting our happiness and joy, we're creating a catalog of story material to choose from when we need it. Like Hansel and Gretel's bread crumbs, that trail of our positive stories can lead us back to good if we've lost our way.

When you come across a story—from memory, via someone else, or some other way—and it is a story that *serves* you, write it down. If it's a story that makes you feel good or makes you want to do better or reminds you of how great you really are, or what you're capable of, *write it down*. Grab your notebook and a pen and ink it. Include the details, include the emotion, include the characters—the components a story needs to be memorable. Our memories are flimsy. When you discover stories that help you break through mental barriers, don't leave it to your memory to recall them when you need them most. Write them down, then periodically go back and reread them to make sure the best ones are staying top of mind.

Get Digital

Changing the stories I told myself before a presentation had a dramatic effect on my life. And though I *did* jot them in a journal at one point, that's not where they started. I wrote one of my stories in the form of a column I used to have at Inc.com. Another I wrote in a blog post. And those were, of course, digital, not handwritten.

Though there is a lot of evidence that writing by hand is valuable, capturing the *story* is what matters most. If you have a weekly newsletter and there is a way to work one of your stories in there, do it. If you have a blog with even a small following, post your story there.

Some of the best stories I tell myself are ones I write for Instagram. If you were to look at my account and read the captions, you would think the posts are for my followers. And they are— but they're also for me. Each one is a little bookmark—a memory trigger for a tiny story that serves. When I get the sense that I have a few stubborn stories holding me back, I open up my Instagram and read the stories of *my own life*. Stories about my work, stories about my kids, stories about my husband, stories about my struggles and what I've overcome. Sure, looking at other people's highlight reels can be intimidating, but looking at your own is inspiring!

If social media is your thing, share your stories there—not only can you go back and revisit them when you need to, but you'll get the added benefit of your social stats increasing because algorithms love stories.

STRATEGY #2: SPEAK YOUR STORIES ALOUD

There's something about *voicing* your story, about speaking it out into the world, that gives it strength. It reinforces the story, makes it official. Research has shown that talking to yourself out loud can help you remember more, motivate you, and reduce self-criticism.[4] Speaking your stories out loud is a powerful exercise; here are a few ways to approach it.

Aloud and Alone

When I prepare a new keynote, I spend a lot of time pacing in my apartment, speaking aloud. I've found that, even if I feel I've written something great, the act of speaking it out loud does something—it's during this period of pacing and talking to the walls that I find some of my best insights. Speaking aloud, I've discovered, is more than just practicing what I say; it's *discovering* what I'll say. That's when the story really comes alive. It's when the unexpected connections appear. And it's when I not only remember what I've forgotten but when I forget about the things I don't need to remember.

Aloud to Someone Else

I have been blessed throughout my life to have people who will listen to my stories. Not just the whine-and-moan, dramatic stories—anyone will listen to those (remember, we love a negative story), but the stories of when I was my most proud, stories of when I was at my best.

My mother was my first audience of one; any story I wanted to tell, she was there to listen. Like when I would come home from middle school in February after broomball in PE, a sport where we ran around on the skating rink in boots and helmets with sticks. I was never much of an athlete, but when it came to broomball, I was *fierce*. I would recount every move to my mother, every block, and every time I got yelled at for being too aggressive. I would walk in the front door after getting off the bus, drop my backpack and take off my hat—my hair a curly mess framing my face (the only time my hair curled like that was a rainy day in summer or playing broomball)—and I would tell my mom the story of broomball, and she would listen to every word of it.

After my mother, there was Maren, my roommate in college and graduate school, and best friend to this day. Every night I would come home from school or from work at the Outback Steakhouse to an open ear, ready to hear all the stories.

And then there is Michael, the ultimate story-listener. Anytime I dig a story up from the depths of an iceberg—good or bad—he is there to listen. With each telling, the stories solidify, and my understanding of what they mean in my life and what lessons I can learn from them crystalizes. With each retelling, I reinforce who I know myself to be.

You likely have a person in your life like this as well—someone you can tell the good stories to. *Do it*. Over dinner, catching up on a call, on a walk—tell your great stories aloud to solidify them in your mind. (And don't be surprised if, after reading this, you suddenly have a deeper appreciation for the story-listeners in your life. What a blessing to have someone to share stories with, good or bad—more on that later.)

Don't forget, too, that sharing even your *search* for stories aloud is a powerful strategy. If you're stuck, fumbling for stories that serve you, *tell someone.* Remember Amie? In chapter 4, she faced a difficult work conversation with an angry customer. In her anxiety about the coming meeting, all she could recall were stories that kept her stuck. Her breakthrough came when she told her husband, "I have to focus on the positive stories. But I can't think of any." It was only by sharing her *need* for stories with someone else that she was able to find them.

Use your voice. That's what it's for.

Share Your Story, Change the World

I have an ulterior motive for writing this book: I want to change the world.

It took me a moment to accept that idea when it first came to mind. I've never been a dent-the-universe kind of person. I remember interviewing Vishen Lakhiani, author of *The Code of the Extraordinary Mind,* and being totally mystified by the way his brain worked. It was like he was operating on a different plane. I knew these people existed—the Elon Musks and Steve Jobses of the world—but I'd never really *talked* to a universe-denter before. That conversation cemented something I had long suspected—universe denting wasn't in my future. That didn't bother me; it was never on my bucket list.

But then I started writing this book. I started intentionally walking people through the method and it worked—the same way it had always worked for me. And while the changes that were happening for each of them were exciting and inspiring, something bigger began to happen. As participants began to share their chosen positive stories with their friends, close family members, partners, and spouses, what started as an exercise quickly transformed into something bigger. Each person who told a positive story gave permission to the listener to revisit, explore, and consider a positive story of their *own*. And something magical began to happen.

My group members shared their stories. Then, people they told their stories to began sharing their *own* stories. And so on. With each telling, a ripple of positive stories vibrated out into the world.

Just imagine what is possible here.

What if *you,* by putting these strategies into practice, share your positive story with someone important to you? And what if they share a positive story in return and, to their surprise (not yours—you know what's happening here), they feel a little better about themselves?

What if they believe in themselves a little more?

Doubt themselves a little less?

And, as a result, they carry that feeling into the rest of their day and *behave* differently. They say yes to a challenging opportunity. They speak up in a meeting. They share their true feelings with an important person in their life.

They step into their greatness just a little bit more. They're kinder to others because they're kinder to themselves.

All because *you* shared *your* story.

This is universe-denting material here, my friend. Sharing your stories has world-changing possibilities. And it begins with you.

Sharing your stories aloud with someone else not only gives you a chance to engage them to help you; telling your story is an invitation for them to share *theirs.* When you share your stories, you send a ripple of positive storytelling out into the world.

STRATEGY #3: PLAN FOR THE TOUGH MOMENTS

Meet Sam.

Every Monday, Sam gets an email.

It's an email he dreads. He wants to avoid it.

The email shows Sam a ranking of the top financial advisors in the company he works for. It tells Sam, at little more than a glance, where he stands in comparison to his peers on the team.

Sam does not want to know this information.

He would like to ignore the email. To *delete* the email. But it's from his boss, so he can't. He needs to at least skim it, click the link.

But that always leads to the same result: Sam feeling terrible. Feeling less than. Feeling average.

This is the cycle of every Monday. Sam dreads email. Sam gets email. Sam reads email. Sam feels lousy.

It wasn't hard for Sam to tease out the clues of a story at work— iceberg statements like *I'm not enough*, *I'm replaceable*, and *I'm just average*. And Sam is an introspective guy. He knows where the stories come from. He's even chosen better stories to help him.

The problem is that email. It's a trigger for Sam. Before he can get a thought in edgewise, that email arrives, and *boom*—Sam's running headlong into the iceberg of *I'm average*.

Weight loss experts will tell you never to buy junk food. If you don't *buy* Oreos, you won't have them in the house during your moments of weakness, and you won't *eat* them. Your best friend will tell you to block the guy who only texts after midnight. Productivity gurus will tell you to delete Facebook, Twitter, TikTok, Instagram (or whatever time-suck app is popular when you read this) to avoid falling down the rabbit hole.

And while these strategies *can* work, there are some triggers you simply can't avoid and others you simply can't resist. Your alarm *will* go off in the morning, and you *will* have a split-second decision to make. Do you get up and work out as you promised yourself you would? Or do you hit snooze? Your manager who acts as if he's God knocks on your office door and sees you sitting at your desk: you're going to have to interact with him. Do you come from a place of empowerment? Or do you fall into a self-doubt tailspin?

Eliminating triggers can be effective, but it will only get you so far. Life is filled will negative-story booby traps that can sneak up and bite you like a snake in the grass. What you need in these situations is antivenom. You need the antidote to negative story triggers. That's what this piece of the installation process is about. It's one thing to build a baseline of positive self-stories. But what happens when you are faced with a direct assault? That's when being ready with your stories matters most.

Once you've chosen a better story, once you've fully told it to yourself and perhaps someone close to you, your next job is to give your new story the best possible chance of success by creating, to borrow from the realm of health psychology, a simple but powerful tool called the *implementation intention*.

Implementation intentions are simple plans that you make, in advance, about how you *intend to act*.

Researchers have found, for example, that someone who says, "Next week, I will exercise vigorously on Tuesday at 10:00 a.m. at the gym," is more than twice as likely to exercise as someone who tries to use simple motivation, like reading about how good exercise is for their health.[5]

You can adapt this tool for your own story purposes using the following formula:

The next time <trigger>, I will say <new story reminder> and tell myself <new story>.

This is the perfect tool for Sam. He's come up with several great stories—one in particular that I really like. We call it the Tree Story.

The Tree Story

Sam remembers his family's ranch in Montana. Sam was a young boy. The ranch was set on a wide-open plain, with little shade—except for around their home. There, his grandfather—also a Sam—had taken the time to plant trees in a large shade belt. The trees kept the place cool in summer and protected it from winter storms.

Sam's dad had praised Grandpa Sam's foresight and the great generosity of doing work when you might not see benefits right away—or ever. The idea stuck with Sam, as did an Asian proverb he'd always liked: *a generation plants a tree in whose shade another generation rests.*

Of course, the Tree Story at first was someone *else's* story—it was really a story of Grandpa Sam. But recently, Sam had planted a tree of his own.

It was innocuous enough, at first. They were cleaning the yard and needed a tree. Off Sam went to Home Depot, picked up a tree, and started digging. No big deal. At first.

"As I was planting the tree, it all came crashing in," he said. "This is something that I've always wanted to do, and here I am. Even if my daughter doesn't sit under the tree, someone else's daughter will."

And things began to change. Sam's story was deeply connected to his values—he could see that immediately. He was doing something so many people *didn't*. Something *important*. Something that wouldn't bear fruit until years into the future. Something for *somebody else*.

Here's what I know: it's impossible to feel like you're doing something important *and* feel average at the same time. I knew this story was Sam's entry point to change. And even though at first it wasn't clear to Sam if this story even counted as one that could be used in his career—he was a financial planner, not a farmer—it didn't take long to realize this story had everything to do with both his career *and* the self-storytelling problem he was facing. While he may not be at the top of the list of new accounts secured each week, he was doing the slow, important, sometimes thankless work of helping people plant financial seeds for future wealth trees.

That was the story Sam decided to use for his implementation intention.

Next time <trigger>, I will say <new story reminder> and tell myself <new story>.

In Sam's case, that Monday email is the trigger. The "Tree Story" is his reminder, and the story is, of course, the Tree Story itself.

Sam *knows* his trigger is coming. He even knows when! When the email arrives, Sam just has to call on the *new*, better story.

Which is exactly what he did.

The following Monday, Sam opened his inbox to find the message from the company honoring the top performers. Before opening it, he took a moment and told himself the Tree Story.

For Sam, the story immediately connects him to his *purpose*—the reason he does what he does. "When we connect with our purpose . . . some of the peripheral stuff, it's still there, but it doesn't matter because I can't see it."

To maximize your stories, identify some of your most vulnerable moments.

- Do you fall into a pit of unworthiness every time you open social media? Tell yourself one of your positive stories as you open the app.
- Does lunch with your mother leave you feeling guilty? Tell yourself one of your positive stories in that moment between putting your car in park and walking up to the host stand.
- Does seeing a call coming in from your condescending boss send you into a state of panic and/or defensiveness—neither of which, you are well aware, are a good look? Tell yourself a chosen story before accepting the call.
- Do you refuse to have sweets in the house but then, as soon as the kids are in bed, you open the delivery app on your phone and order a cookie from Levain Bakery even though the cookie weighs three pounds and costs $11.00 and you swear you'll split it with your husband, but then he blinks, and you devour the whole thing yourself and pretend it never happened? (Hypothetically speaking, of course.)

(If that last one, hypothetically, resonates with you, might I suggest that the moment you feel the urge to open the app, instead tell yourself the story of the time you had been making better decisions for your health and went to that friend's backyard wedding with your husband, and felt so free, and light, and happy, and beautiful. Then pay close attention to the feeling that washes over you as you put your phone down and turn on an old episode of *The Office* instead of ordering the cookie.)

Of course, for this to work, you must first identify what some of your triggers are. A few of the most common offenders include but are not limited to: certain people, times of day, social media, states of being (overly tired, overly hungry, dehydrated, overcaffeinated), recurring events. Additionally, while there are times when you can see a trigger coming a mile away, other times they can catch you off guard. In the case of the latter, once the trigger has passed and before you do anything else, tell yourself some of your chosen stories to stop the bleeding and get you back on your chosen path.

STRATEGY #4: START YOUR DAY WITH STORIES THAT SERVE YOU

Perhaps the most important strategy for changing your life through choosing better stories is starting each day by reminding yourself of the stories that serve you. Read over them quickly. Retell them during your morning workout or on your commute to work. Revisit them as you stand in the shower or while you wait for your first cup of coffee to brew. It doesn't have to be overly involved. Once you've fully remembered and documented the story, it may only take a keyword to bring the details forward.

Post-it Progress

Meet Will.

Even via Zoom from his basement, I could tell that he was a life-of-the-party guy. He was also a loving husband, devoted father, and successful business owner.

As you might imagine, all those things had taken time. So much time that he never rode his spin bike that stood in the basement a mere five feet from his desk. When he *did* go into the office, he never had time to pack a healthy lunch, so he would just pick something up from one of the fast-food places in his office complex.

You can see where this story is going.

Will's behaviors weren't adding up to the kind of life he wanted to live, but his efforts to change had proven futile. That's how we came together; Will wanted to take a real shot at changing his story.

Will is a straightforward guy. Like any of us, he was struggling to take what he *knew* and use it to do what he needed to *do* to cross the gap.

Will found the story that worked. It was a short one. A simple tale. (Remember, a story doesn't have to be a masterpiece in order to get the job done.) It happened several years earlier when Will was putting in the lifestyle work and had reached a healthy weight. He was walking down the hallway in his office when a colleague he respected stopped him and said, "Hey, Will, you look really great. Keep up the good work, brother."

Will could tell the man was legitimately impressed and, for reasons he couldn't quite explain, that compliment just felt *so good*. It was the ultimate expression of his hard work paying off. And Will wanted that feeling again.

We were both confident that telling himself that story would help him:

- step away from work at a reasonable hour to make time to ride his spin bike each day.
- plan ahead and always have healthy options to bring to work and eat at home.
- get him back on track if he had an off weekend.

But how to remember the plan?

Every morning, the first thing Will did when he woke up was go into the bathroom, open the medicine cabinet, and grab his toothbrush. To keep the story of his colleague supporting his efforts front of mind, Will wrote down the guy's name on a Post-it and taped it inside the door of his medicine cabinet.

Now, when he brushed his teeth, he wasn't just supporting his dental health; he was improving his mental health as well. There, staring him right in the eye, was the reminder of the story of the feeling he was working toward.

I caught up with Will a few weeks after first incorporating the story reminder in his daily activity. I had my pen ready with high hopes of capturing the amazing details of his transformation.

"I just did it." That was all he said.

"You just . . . did it . . . ?" I repeated.

"Yeah. I read the note, remembered the story, and I just did it."

I told you Will was a straightforward guy.

After years of insisting it was his calendar's fault that he couldn't work out, everything changed *overnight*. Like, actually overnight. He saw the note the next morning, he remembered the story and the feeling, and he changed. Just like that.

Will went to the grocery store with a plan. He scheduled his workouts. He took advantage of breaks.

"The other day," he said, "I noticed I had a spare hour in between two meetings, so I hopped on the bike quick and got my workout in." He paused. "Yep, that's it. That's what I've been doing."

And that was it. Straightforward Will, laying his yellow brick road.

Post-it notes. Rubber bands. Reminders. However you do it, start your day with your chosen stories to remind yourself who you truly are. Review them with your morning coffee or think them through on your way home from dropping your kids off at school. Commit to telling yourself the stories that serve you—this is how you make them *louder* and *stronger* than the stories that hold you back.

OLD STORIES DIE HARD

I would be remiss to mention, as you might have already guessed, that old stories, of course, don't always *want* to be changed.

Recently, I was helping my daughter during the independent work portion of her third-grade virtual writing class. She was getting extremely frustrated, and I could tell the story in her sweet little head was, "I can't do this."

Now, I'll admit the environment was less than ideal. Trying to write while staring at a Zoom screen with twenty other third-graders unmuting themselves and chiming in is tough. But I also knew she was a great writer, and I knew that she knew it, too.

At that moment, however, she had let a different story take over.

During lunch, we took a moment to talk about her writing struggle. We discussed how she was feeling during the assignment, and she shared those definitive statements that are textbook self-storytelling hooks. "I'm not a good writer." "I don't know how to write a story." "I can never think of anything to write about."

These stories sound *so* convincing. It doesn't matter if you're eight years old or eighty—it's easy to get caught in a downward spiral. We needed a replacement story, stat!

After listening to my daughter's concerns, I gently asked if she remembered the award she had won at the end of the previous school year. She looked at me blankly at first, and then her expression gradually changed as she recalled the "Best Writer" certificate she received. I added to the story, helping her recall the day, how proud her teachers were of her, and how proud she was of herself and all her hard work.

Still, old stories die hard. Stories that don't serve us often dig in deeper when they sense their hold on us is being threatened.

"But," she protested, "they just gave that to me because *you* are a writer." I gently reminded her of all the different things she wrote about last year—the dolphin book, the many stories she wrote about a character named Violet. The how-to book about ballet. I shared story after story after story that illustrated her ability to write, and with each one, I could see the new story gaining control.

The next writing session, she sat down, and I watched as the words practically flew off the tip of her pencil and onto the page.

The lesson here is to *expect your existing stories to be tenacious*. They are neural habits. They're wired in. They have a foothold, and frankly, they don't want to give it up, thank you very much.

New stories will eventually weaken the hold of your old ones, but don't expect to wake up one morning, have an epiphany, and change everything in your life that day. (Unless you're Will.)

Instead, expect a *process*. Expect it to be not easy—but also not impossible. The same thing that helped you create the old story is the very same thing that's going to help you create the *new* one. You're not doing anything you don't already know how to do. You're just going to do it deliberately.

But don't be discouraged if your old stories hang around. They may always be there. Even when I've replaced a story that doesn't serve me, I prefer to think of my old stories as a part of me. They're like an old photograph of a bad haircut that I can point to and say, "That was me once, but it's not me anymore."

Until you completely habituate a new story, your old one is going to run in your head, at least some of the time. In fact, it might *always* run. The game is to catch it in action and scare it off—like spying a rare animal as it slinks off in the dark.

It's hard to override a negative story with a newer, more fragile version. The key is to tell this new story louder and to tell it over and over and over again. Your old story might leap into action at the first sign of stress. But that doesn't mean you can't interrupt it with your carefully planned *new* story and change the path ahead.

STORIES ABOUT STORIES

Change the path ahead. There's no better phrase to describe what happened with workshop participants (and if you're interested in participating in a version of that experience, visit www.chooseyourstorychangeyourlife.com/resources for all the options available to you). With each positive story they chose and installed, their lives seemed to become more vibrant, more purposeful, more *theirs*.

What was most apparent with each passing day, however, was how valuable it was to hear *other* stories. To see real examples of people who had changed their relationships, their professional lives, or their financial situations. People who had become better parents, better partners, better friends. People who transformed their health or their business.

Those stories mattered to more than just the people who told them; they mattered to the people who *heard* them. They made choosing better stories real. They made choosing better stories *possible*.

Those stories are what I want to share with you next.

PART III

HACKING YOUR ESSENTIAL STORIES

Tales of Transformation

BUSINESS AND CAREER

Choosing Your Own Success Story Adventure

*You're writing the story as you go. Seeing all of that
and putting it all together, it's like I can dream again. I
can see the future.*

— HEATHER

Meet Samantha Ponder.

Of course, if you're a sports fan, it's possible you already know Samantha—or at least you've seen her either as host of *Sunday NFL Countdown* on ESPN or, prior to that, as a reporter for both college football and college basketball on ESPN. Samantha is sharp, composed, and, most important, knows ball.

The daughter of a coach and longtime lover of sports, Samantha knew at a young age that, though she wouldn't necessarily make a living *playing* sports, maybe there was another way—maybe she could be on the radio talking about sports. Maybe she could write about sports. Maybe she could announce for the Phoenix Suns, her hometown basketball team. She didn't have a specific plan except to stay as close to sports as much as she could.

Then, her senior year of high school, Samantha won a speech-writing contest and the prize was reading the speech at graduation in front of thousands of people. "I remember my principal introducing me right before I gave my speech and saying something like, 'In five years you'll see Samantha on ESPN . . .'" Samantha's family didn't even have cable in their home, much less ESPN and she had never really dreamed of anything that big. "In hindsight it was almost like she was calling me out." And it worked. Samantha quickly moved from the sidelines to the main stage, and on any given Sunday you can see her hard work at play.

Recently, a documentary was released about the history of one of the programs Samantha was a part of. One of Samantha's colleagues was asked about her during his interview. He had mostly only positive things to say . . . things like, "Sam really knows ball," and how she's there for the game and not for the fame—all very good things. "But then there was *one thing*," Samantha mentioned. "One little statement, not even a full sentence really and it wasn't even that bad . . . but he said, 'She's a little quirky,' and suddenly I was questioning everything!"

Am I quirky? she wondered.

What does he *mean* by quirky? she wondered.

Is quirky a *bad* thing? she wondered.

Do *other* people think I'm quirky? she wondered.

As a public figure, and especially as one of a handful of females in a male-dominated industry, Ponder has had plenty of experience with criticism from random people on the internet. One of her many admirable qualities, a quality she's developed over time, is her ability to take those comments in stride or ignore them completely. But this was different. This was a man with whom she'd worked, someone she respected, not a random internet troll.

"I'm surprised at how much that one statement impacted how I thought of myself as a professional."

SELF-STORIES AT WORK AT WORK

My first book, *Stories That Stick*, was all about storytelling in business. It was right there in the subtitle: *How Storytelling Can Captivate Customers, Influence Audiences, and Transform Your Business.* I wrote about the four essential stories everyone in business needs to be able to tell. Storytelling in sales, storytelling in marketing, storytelling in leadership . . . *oh my*! It was all in there. I detailed the importance of storytelling in interviews and presentations and in developing your own personal brand whether you are an entrepreneur or building that brand as you rise through the ranks of an organization. And while there is much more to say about each of those, I would be remiss not to mention that, yes, even in business, the most important stories aren't the ones we carefully craft and tell outwardly. The most important stories are the ones we tell ourselves.

Go ahead and create the most incredible marketing story or tell an amazing opening story in your next sales pitch, but if you leave unattended negative stories to their own devices or leave *out* the positive stories of what you're truly made of, you're building castles on shifting sand. Professional success and fulfillment are built from the inside out, one story at a time.

Fortunately for Samantha Ponder, she's naturally a pretty experienced self-storyteller. She started dismantling her icebergs years ago, which is likely part of the reason she is where she is. After her initial reaction to the comment about her quirkiness, Ponder did some . . . well . . . pondering, and came to a conclusion that you've likely come to through the course of reading this book: that within each of us is a lifetime of stories—these stories shape the way we see the world. And *because* each of us has within us a lifetime of stories, there is no possible way we could possibly understand every single nuance of another human being because there is no possible way to know all of their stories when we can barely get a handle on our own. "It's arrogant to try," she said.

And, ultimately, *why* try? We have very little control over the stories others tell about us and yet a lot of professional time is wasted on trying to figure out what other people think when, instead, we should be focusing on the stories we actually *can* change—the ones we tell ourselves.

This chapter is dedicated to helping you reallocate that time—instead of focusing on the stories outside you or around you, to focus on the stories with*in* you to advance your professional aspirations. Of course, in order to gain control of your stories, you have to catch them first.

STEP ONE: CATCH YOUR STORIES AT WORK

"I'm not good enough." "No one respects my ideas." "My boss hates me." "They never acknowledge my hard work." "I've just been lucky so far." "That's just not possible for me." When it comes to self-stories in the office, the tips of the icebergs come in many shapes and sizes.

If you don't speak up in a meeting and regret it afterward, there is likely a self-story there. If you find yourself overthinking inter-actions at a networking dinner or cocktail hour, there's probably a self-story there. Use these moments of second-guessing (some-times even cringing), as clues to uncovering deeper self-stories.

Is This Making Sense So Far?

In a conversation with Eliza VanCort, author of the book *A Woman's Guide to Claiming Space,* she highlighted the phrases women in particular use when they feel unsure. Statements like, "Do you know what I mean?" and "Does that make sense?" and even the very brief, "Right?" permeate professional conversations of all kinds and are dead giveaways for self-doubt.

And where there is self-doubt, there is a self-story.

If ever you catch yourself saying one of these phrases, it's likely you've also caught a self-story iceberg. Make a mental note in the moment and commit to revisiting it once the communication event or presentation is complete.

Your Future's in the Feedback

One of the most important professional trainings I ever received hap-pened long before I put on a pair of heels and a blazer—it was in high school, on the speech team, and not for the reason you might think. Because while, yes, the speech team inoculated me from the fear of public speaking, more importantly, it set me up to receive feedback. Every meet, you give your speech at least three different times, to three different judges and an audience of your competitors. After the speech, you are handed a sheet of paper where the judge writes down in detail what you did well, and *extreme* detail what you could improve (or, more often than not, what was bad). Aside from a few rogue judges, most of the feedback was constructive in nature. But even the most judicious feedback can sting, and I remember many occasions when a feedback form shook me to my core and left me fuming, furious, and cursing the fool who said I looked like I was going to pass out, I was talking so fast . . .

Except, I *did* talk too fast.

And if I wanted to achieve my goals—namely, winning—I really was going to have to slow down.

The same is true in the professional world. One of the easiest ways to catch your self-stories in the act is to pay close attention to feedback—both the feedback you receive and how you respond to it.

First, the feedback itself. If you're told you need to be more of a team player, you may be operating from a set of stories where in childhood you were rewarded for being the best, not for being part of a collective success. Or perhaps years in an individual sales role at a cutthroat company conditioned you to go for the win no matter who you take out in the process, but now you're working in a completely different company culture where teamwork is more highly regarded.

One executive at a large international firm stated that when it comes to improvement conversations they are almost exclusively about communication. "Being more planned, more structured, and more thoughtful in both written and oral communication." For those looking to rise through the ranks, male or female, deliberate communication was almost always the path forward. This feedback is an opportunity to explore what self-stories might be encouraging you or at the very least giving you permission to craft messages on a whim. Maybe you're the oldest in your family and so were never really questioned. Perhaps you were a big fish in a small pond and could get by on talent and charm alone . . . but now you're one of many, many big talented charming fish and so excellence is going to require more.

Feedback itself can be an excellent prompt to catch the stories that are promoting certain behaviors that are now working against you.

Second, while the feedback itself is important, when it comes to using it as a tool for catching your invisible self-stories, your *response* to feedback is equally as valuable.

For example, an executive at a Fortune 500 company was struggling with one of her direct reports. The manager was extremely good at her job, hit all of her targets, and yet every time someone offered her feedback, she started crying. "The manager will storm out of meetings and slam the door. She'll burst into tears on a Zoom call and turn off her camera. . . It's really a problem." The executive has had many direct conversations about this situation with the manager and has offered several solutions. "She's driven and motivated and has her sights set on a promotion." The executive shook her head. "But until she can handle feedback, I just don't see that in her future."

Constructive feedback can be tough to take. It can make us mad, sad (this is starting to sound like a *Sesame Street* episode), jealous, furious, vengeful (that's better). It can make our cheeks flush, our lip quiver, our heart rate pick up, and yes . . . even make us cry. And while I believe composure is a virtue, a lack thereof is also an opportunity. Paying attention to your response *to* feedback can be a dead giveaway for stories that are holding you back. Crying might signal stories in your past about perfectionism. Anger might signal stories of when you felt slighted or overlooked. Constructive feedback is a reality of professional progress and now it can also be a tool for catching self-stories in the act.

STEP TWO: ANALYZE YOUR SELF-STORIES

Meet Tammy.

Tammy is interested in starting a new job. She is several years into her career in digital marketing and, though she enjoys her job, she's reached the top of her current company's ranks and is ready to take on a new challenge elsewhere. The market is hot right now for people with her particular skill set and she's recently moved to a new city where there are a lot of great businesses looking for someone like her.

And yet, she's paralyzed.

Logically, it makes perfect sense for her to put herself out there a little. She has nothing to lose and everything to gain. "I just can't seem to *do* anything." And so, she doesn't. And it's beginning to eat away at her. Why?! Why won't she just send her resume to someone?

Then she realized, it's because of a story. The story is from many years ago—a different time when she moved to a new city and began the hunt for a new job. She went into the search confident. After all, she had experience and the glowing references to back it up. However, after weeks of searching and many, many interviews, all she heard was *no*. One particularly devastating week she received nine rejections. Eventually, she found a great job and even ended up working on several projects for some of the very same companies who rejected her. But the emotions of shame and fear, even years later, have stuck with her and are still alive and well.

In chapter 5, I shared the six questions to ask yourself when analyzing your self-stories. Question #2 was: *Is this story true?* Sometimes the answer is no, but sometimes the answer is, unfortunately, yes. It was true, Tammy had been rejected many, many times during her job search. It could be true that, yes, you got laid off in a recent round of cutbacks. It could be true that, yes, you were just plain fired or let go on some unpleasant terms. The path to professional success is rarely a straight line. It includes ups and downs and lateral moves and often has a few blips or breaks in the timeline. It is reported that over 90 percent of working people report a period of unemployment.[1]

Yes, sometimes the stories *are* true and they're not pretty, which means coming to terms with those stories if you desire professional advancement. Not sugarcoating it, not pretending it isn't there. Not putting lipstick on it. But rather accepting it and then leaving it where it belongs . . . in the past. And then begin the process of choosing a better story.

STEP THREE: CHOOSE A STORY THAT SERVES YOU

Meet Heather.

Heather lives in Pennsylvania. She's a wife, a mother to four kids—a full-time job on its own—and she's also a budding entrepreneur who is working on a side hustle and has crazy goals and even bigger dreams. Which, when it comes to side hustles and entrepreneurship, "crazy goals" and "bigger dreams" is basically a requirement. And yet . . . she's noticed a problem. Her business isn't where she wants it to be and the goals only seem to be making it worse. "Having these goals and not living up to them," she told me, "that's really hard for me. I have huge goals for my business and I'm four years in and I'm barely breaking the surface."

It would be fair to say that *everyone* feels that way at times about their work (and many don't have four kids). After all, who doesn't want their business to grow? Who doesn't wish for a bigger paycheck each week, or brighter career prospects? But the problem for Heather was that the gap between where she is and where she wants to be seemed to have taken on a larger-than-life role. It seemed to be getting bigger instead of smaller. It was almost as if Heather was going *backward*. Rather than spurring her on and inspiring her to move forward, her business goals and visualizing and dreaming seemed to be making things *worse*.

This idea of goals leading us astray may sound counter to everything you've been taught about moving forward in your professional life. The way to success, we're taught, is to dream big. To set goals. To have targets. "Begin with the end in mind," we're told. Or, "Shoot for the moon! Even if you miss, you'll end up among the stars."

This pithy (and astronomically impossible) wisdom isn't entirely wrong. Goals are a good thing, and they *do* have a purpose, particularly at work. However, it turns out, goals have a dark side that is worth mentioning.

Vision Bored

If you can dream it . . . then your brain may think you've already done it?

That, apparently, can happen.

If you've been making vision boards, and spending hours and hours envisioning your goals in detail, there is some evidence that this kind of vivid, future-based thinking can backfire.

In one study, researchers tracked the progress of participants trying to find a fulfilling job. Those who spent the most time fantasizing about their future fulfilling work actually applied for fewer jobs, got fewer offers, and when they did get work, got paid less![2]

The problem with all this future-think is that it can actually undermine our attempts to *do the actual work*. Some researchers believe that excessive visualization might trick a part of your brain into thinking you've already reached the goal, thereby reducing your motivation to do the work.

Journey vs. Destination

Just because goals work doesn't mean that increasing them will continue to deliver good results. As researchers behind the study

"Goals Gone Wild" discovered, too much goal setting can lead to unintended consequences.[3] When we obsess over goals, we might cut corners, or behave unethically. We get tunnel vision, where the goal becomes the only thing we can see.[4]

And therein lies the problem with tunnel vision: too much focus on destination means not enough energy acknowledging and honoring the stories of the journey. The end result of goals gone wild is *feeling bad*. Which is exactly where Heather was. Her goals were placing her focus on how far she is from where she wants to be. Her Super Shiny Future Self is so bright and successful and amazing that her present self—well, her present self just felt a little dull in comparison. How could it not?

Just like all of the participants in the self-storytelling project, Heather's job for our third session together was to come with a set of stories she could tell herself that *served* her. Stories that refocused her attention to the journey, to the progress, to the success she *has* achieved instead of what she hasn't. Heather admitted it was much easier to find the negative stories than the positive ones at first; yes, I'll say it again, that's the negative bias at work—making our down moments stand out in our memories, making them vivid and easier to recall. "The common thread in all those negative stories, though," Heather noticed, "was I was focusing on my own lack, my own failure. They were times when I didn't feel like I was enough or I didn't make the cut, or that I failed."

That gave her an idea. What is the opposite of these negative stories? Stories of when she *was* enough. Stories of when she *did* make the cut. Stories of when she *succeeded*. "All of my best stories, my most successful moments, were when I was focusing on what I was giving instead of what I didn't have . . ."

And there it was. Her best stories were about what she had and what she'd done—not about where she was going or what she was missing.

Heather found the story of when she achieved one of the ranks she'd been aiming for. "I remember telling my husband—he picked me up and twirled me around in the kitchen. He was like, 'I'm so excited for you; I'm so proud of you.'" It was a story that had been lost completely in the haze and fury of her goals.

She remembered the day she found out she had earned one of the company sales trips. "Even though the trip got canceled because of the pandemic, that doesn't make the fact that I earned it any less amazing."

Heather remembered the story of a family vacation they were able to take because of the extra income she'd earned with her side hustle. "I remember the day we left and how happy I felt—I *did* this! I made this happen for our family."

Once she started actively looking for them, these stories were everywhere. And while she didn't suddenly achieve her big, crazy goals and dreams, she felt a lot better about what she *had* achieved, which made her feel better about what was to come, and for now, that was an important step.

By our last session, it was like I was talking to a different Heather. "I just feel capable and excited," she said. "It's been a couple of weeks, but the way that I feel is completely shifted." When I repeated back some of Heather's iceberg statements—the little clues to the stories beneath, like, "I'm not good enough,"—I could almost see her flinch a little. "Cringy," she says. "But that's honestly where I was . . . that's how I felt. I knew that I didn't want to feel that way, but I also didn't quite know how to *not* feel that way."

It sounds so simple, doesn't it?

And yet who among us hasn't had phases of life where we've felt bad about where we are instead of where we should be or discouraged by the potential we haven't lived up to? Potential can be a cruel master, and goals have a way of highlighting its power. Potential is fleeting. It's ambiguous. By definition, you never quite reach it. Skills enable new skills. Accomplishments enable newer, larger accomplishments. Confidence begets greater confidence. Your potential is an ever-moving signpost that is wonderful for helping you grow, but terrible if you never celebrate that growth by looking back at the stories that show you just how far you've come. Choosing the right stories and putting them on repeat helps shore up the flaws that are inherently wired into goals, and as a result, wired into our professional lives.

The last thing Heather did in our final meeting was take a picture of the screen of our Zoom call, our two smiling faces looking at each other across a few hundred miles.

"Gotta have a memory," she said with a laugh. It'll make a good story.

STEP FOUR: INSTALL YOUR CHOSEN STORIES

When it comes to installing your chosen stories in business, the options are endless.

One woman in the group had a story ready anytime her condescending boss approached her cubicle (by the end of our sessions, she had left her job and was starting her own company with her husband). One man in the group told himself his stories just before stepping into meetings, virtual or in person, with key donors. One woman told herself her stories right before she opened her social media accounts and again right afterward. You read in chapter 7 how I installed stories right before I took the stage. Tammy can tell herself the stories anytime she feels hesitant about sending her resume. Heather can tell herself the stories anytime she starts to feel anxious about the progress she's made.

Professional life is rich with opportunities for installing better self-stories. Here are a few situations where it is particularly important.

The Story You Tell Yourself About Why You Can't

Meet Julie.

Julie has more energy than a brand-new puppy, more positivity than the top of a Duracell battery, and defies all laws of gravity and nature with her wrinkle-free face and ageless physique. Julie is a health and fitness coach and has been teaching fitness classes since long before virtual instruction was a twinkle in Peloton's eye. She leaps through life in spandex and makes you feel like you could, too, and in fact you *should*. Julie's professional dream? To build her fitness and coaching empire. Seems reasonable, right? Especially after the little you already know of her and yes, she is well on her way. But though Julie desires this and despite the fact that all signs point toward her innate ability to achieve this goal, if you were to really ask Julie, she'd tell you she can't do it. Why? According to Julie, she *can't* achieve that professional goal because she is too old.

Yes. The woman who could be twenty-three or fifty-three would tell you, "I got started too late. There are too many people younger than me who want to do the same thing. I'm too old." If you pressed further, Julie would tell you plenty of stories to make you (and herself) believe the story she's telling herself.

Julie is not the only one with a story about why she can't . . . There's also Mark. Mark started in the warehouse of a company affixing labels to boxes and eventually worked his way to becoming a senior member of the accounting team. But if you were to ask him, he'll tell you he can't actually *do* accounting. Why? Because he doesn't have his CPA. Or Sara. Sara who has years of community organizing and activism experience and a strong desire to run for office but *can't*. Why? You guessed it. Because she's never run for office before. Try to tell her that every elected official had to run for office the first time and she still won't believe that she can.

The first place to start installing better stories is anytime you find yourself telling a story of why you *can't*. This is the low-hanging fruit and it helps to approach it with a sense of humor because, let's face it, the stories we tell ourselves, which turn into the reasons we give ourselves, can be downright ridiculous. Swapping out these stories for ones that serve you is the first step in moving to the next level.

The Story You Tell Yourself About What You Have and Haven't Achieved

I sometimes think about Ryan Lochte, the American competitive swimmer. He made international headlines after a scandal in Brazil following the 2016 Olympics. The charges were later dropped, but not before a significant suspension and millions in lost sponsorships and respect. Lochte has messed up in some pretty significant ways, and while there is no excuse for his behavior, I can't help but wonder if he is perhaps the ultimate example of what happens when we only tell ourselves the story of our professional success in the context of someone else's.

For all of his many, major missteps, Lochte is otherworldly in the water. Specializing in the individual medley, one of the toughest to train for because it requires excellence in not one but all four strokes, he is almost unbeatable. Ryan has earned twelve Olympic medals, six of them gold, and has held multiple world records. He is the "second-most decorated male swimmer in Olympic history measured by total number of medals."[5]

Second only to Michael Phelps.

Yes. Michael Phelps. You knew I couldn't talk about American swimming without mentioning his name—to do so would be sacrilege.

But think about that for a moment, from Lochte's perspective. Imagine if Phelps had been born a decade after Lochte instead of a year. Imagine if Michael Phelps had been a track star or a figure skater instead.

Ryan Lochte would be the phenom.

Ryan Lochte would be the face of Olympic greatness.

Ryan Lochte would be considered the GOAT of swimming and maybe beyond.

We can argue all day about which comes first—the chicken of skill or the egg of attitude. And certainly the absence of Phelps doesn't automatically equate to Lochte, King of the Pool, but I would venture to guess a part of his pattern of self-destruction is the result of the stories Lochte tells himself while in the broad-shouldered shadow of his teammate.

Can you blame him? And if you have ever struggled with accepting and enjoying your own professional success, are you really that different from him? Perhaps you've set a goal and reached it, but instead of celebrating, you immediately remembered the *bigger* goal a colleague or competitor achieved. Have a friend or family member congratulate you on a promotion but you brush it off, thinking about how much longer it took you than someone else.

One of the women in the self-storytelling group shared with me her struggle with her former partner. They had separated on fully amicable terms; her partner was moving across the country and it didn't make sense to keep working together. The woman was sad to see her partner go, but also excited about what was possible on her own. She did some great work, made great progress, secured great clients, and was feeling pretty great about it all. And then she heard about that former partner who had decided to go into a different field completely, struck gold, and was making in a month what she had set as a goal to make in a year. All the things that seemed so great, suddenly, by comparison, weren't so great anymore.

"By comparison" is the operative phrase here.

If ever you are struggling with what you've achieved vs. what you haven't, take a moment to put your achievements in a vacuum. Separate them from the story of anyone else's success. Look at them all on their own, tell them, retell them if only to yourself, and see if they feel different to you. Sometimes we need the reminder to focus just on the glitter of your *own* gold and let that be enough.

The Story You Tell Yourself About Change and the Unknown

Payal Kadakia is the founder and creator of ClassPass, a company that started as a way to conglomerate all of the various fitness and dance studios in any given area into one place for easy access to class times. In January of 2020, ClassPass was valued at over a billion dollars in its latest round of funding. Of course, for a company built almost entirely around in-person fitness, 2020 quickly turned from the year the unicorn spent dancing on rainbows to the year the unicorn faced the impending collapse of its entire world into a fiery pit of destruction and despair. Things were changing rapidly—spiraling, really—it would be enough to shake any founder to her core. Fortunately for Kadakia, she had a story. One of the key stories *any* entrepreneur, though they're valuable for intrapreneurs as well, needs to have. The story about change and the unknown.

Payal remembers it like yesterday. She'd been long living a double life. Successful businesswoman with an extremely prestigious role at a top New York City firm by day, woman with a revolutionary tech idea to solve a pain point by night. After struggling with the decision for herself and the added pressure of what her parents would say, she couldn't keep her desire to leave her job to herself anymore.

"I remember that Thanksgiving. I was home and I told my parents that, you know, I just didn't want to go back to work on Monday." Even when she said it, Kadakia wasn't fully committed to building a company. But then her mother looked at her—her mother who had immigrated to the United States and had always wished for her daughter to have a stable career. "She looked at me and told me to quit." There was still disbelief in her voice as Payal told me the story. "'I think you should quit,' she told me. She said she believed in me, that I'd proven myself, checked every single box that was out there: I had gone to a good school. I had gotten a great career and she basically said, this is the time. If you're going to do it, go bet on yourself and build something." Kadakia thought about her mother's words for a while and eventually mustered up the courage to quit her job, which is a very hard thing for anyone to do.

"I always think back to that day," she said with a quiet knowing in her voice. "I remember walking through the big glass doors of the skyscraper office, afraid. I knew I was going to quit, and I had no idea what was on the other side."

She arrived at her office, turned in her resignation, and sent an email to the entire company explaining that she was leaving and why. Shortly after, she received a call from one of the vice chairmen of the entire company. "He asked that I come to his office," she said, admitting she was a little anxious. "When I got there, he asked to know more about what I was starting, and when I told him, he wrote me a check on the spot. He wanted to invest in the company I hadn't even started yet."

That story became Payal's default mentality. Now, whenever she is faced with fear and uncertainty, she remembers the fear she felt walking through the doors and into the unknown and the even greater excitement she had as she walked out. She tells herself the story of that day as a reminder that you never know the greatness that is waiting just on the other side of fear.

WHAT SUCCESS *REALLY* IS

In the spring of 2020, I took on the role of Chief Storytelling Officer at *SUCCESS* magazine and as part of that role I started the podcast *Success Stories with Kindra Hall* where I interviewed some truly incredible people to hear their stories—how they got to where they are now and, for many of them, what success means to them. Here are a few of their responses:

- Daymond John, founder and CEO of the fashion brand FUBU and a recurring shark on the show *Shark Tank,* said success is "the ability to challenge yourself and live with the decisions that you made, whether you fail or succeed during those challenges."
- Chris Gardner, whose life story was made into the major motion picture *The Pursuit of Happyness* starring Will Smith, mentioned being able to do work that reflects his values and now helping others to believe in and achieve their dreams. (He

also added that, most importantly, he is "the world's greatest grandfather.")

- Tarek El Moussa, real estate investor and star of the reality show *Flip or Flop*, said: "Success is a feeling that I'm chasing every single day . . . [it's] not a number, it's not an object . . . it's a feeling."

- Jamie Kern Lima, American entrepreneur, *New York Times* best-selling author, and one of *Forbes*'s Richest Self-Made Women in America, says that success means knowing that what you're doing is something bigger than yourself. "There are so many people that I know personally that have so much money and such a great resume and so many accolades and billions of dollars. . . I don't believe they're successful if they're not filled with joy and doing something that is bigger than themselves and of service to others."[6]

Several other themes emerged when asked about the definition of success—mainly that success isn't the having-of-things ("How many houses can you live in at one time?!" Gardner joked), but rather something much less tangible. And also, that their definition of success has changed over time. That, years ago, it was one thing but now, after experience and wisdom, it's something different. I found these definitions helpful, insightful, and something I'd been suspicious of. At the time of the interviews, I was redefining the term *success* in my own life. I sensed that the stories I was telling myself weren't really working anymore and that even though I was laying the yellow bricks, I was a little confused about what my final destination was . . . and then I realized, just as the people I had interviewed mentioned, it had changed.

I've always been a hustler—and if you're a hardworking, goal-driven achiever, this might sound familiar to you, too. Over summer break in high school, I worked the morning shift as a beer cart girl on the golf course, the afternoon shift at the local video store (be kind, rewind), and the evening shift as a waitress at a drive-in restaurant.

In grad school, I was a TA teaching multiple Communications 101 classes a week, writing my thesis, working as a manager at the Outback Steakhouse, and working the late shift at the karaoke bar where my acts included a *Grease* medley, a "Love Shack" duet, and something from Britney Spears (until my students caught wind and came to see me perform and then I had to quit).

When I started my own business, I hustled even harder. Two kids? No big deal. Moving every two years? No problem. Every New Year's Eve I set huge revenue goals, trying to outdo the year before. Hustling has been an integral part of my identity—work harder, run faster, push myself to the limit—and in many ways, it's served me.

When Michael and I sat down to establish our goals for 2020, the ambition was no different. We had achieved a *huge* goal in 2019 and I decided to aim for *double*. I hit the ground running—I was only home about ten nights total the first eight weeks of the year. And while it was amazing, and while I was on track for our crazy goal, I found myself asking:

Why?

Why did I need double? What was missing from my life that required double the revenue?

The truth was, the only thing missing from my life . . . was *me*.

I was so caught up in the art and the act of the hustle, I was missing out on the beautiful life it created. My friends, my family, my home . . . what good was any of it if I was too busy hustling to enjoy it?

For the first time in my life, even *before* the pandemic hit, I put a pause on the hustle. I took a long enough breath to examine my life and realized . . . it was everything I wanted. Success was all around me. All I needed to do was see it for what it is.

Make no mistake, the stories you tell yourself about your career and professional success will have an impact. You will see shifts and changes and exciting things will happen. As you lay each yellow brick, your path will progress forward. Just make sure you know the address of your Emerald City, or at least the zip code, so you end up in the right place.

9

HEALTH AND WELL-BEING

Finding Your Stories of True Health

There is no separation between mind and body.

— DEEPAK CHOPRA

Meet Zara.

There's a good chance you already know her, though. Everyone knows Zara. And, though it would seem statistically impossible, every single person who *knows* Zara, *adores* Zara. Mentioning her name in a conversation mandates a two-minute detour (at least) while the parties exchange the variety of ways and reasons that Zara is simply the best. This admiration is universal and knows no boundaries. Her professional contacts adore her; her friends feel blessed to be on group chats with her. Even my son has had a deep, soulful love of Zara ever since the time in second grade when she sat with him on the bus on a field trip; a twenty-minute discussion about collector coins and crystals, and the connection was sealed.

That's just who Zara is. She is one of the good ones. And while you don't want bad things to happen to *anyone,* and certainly not to *good* people, something bad happening to Zara seems to violate laws as deep as the earth's core and as broad as the galaxy we inhabit.

And then one Friday in February, Zara sat in the elementary school auditorium with her husband, Jonathan, and their seven-week-old baby. They were watching their second-grade daughter and first-grade son dance in the school's hip-hop performance.

There is nothing quite like watching a couple hundred kids in color-coded T-shirts show off their dance skills—it was joyful, light-hearted, and exactly what this new mother of three needed. Jonathan needed it, too. Ever since the final weeks of the pregnancy, Jonathan, a talented, energetic CMO of a global brand, hadn't been himself. He'd come home from work and pass out on the couch. After delivery, he slept through much of the rest of the time in the hospital. "I'm all about equality," Zara said, "but I'm sorry. Giving birth is simply *not* as exhausting for the man as it is for the woman, and there he was, sleeping deeply on the hospital couch."

For the sake of their marriage (there's nothing like a husband sleeping all day after his wife has been up all night with a newborn), they decided he should get checked out. "I was convinced he was anemic," Zara said. "He was convinced he contracted dengue fever from a mosquito bite he got on a weekend away in the Hamptons."

Whatever it was, Jonathan had visited his doctor the day before the school performance to get some blood work done, if for no other reason than to settle the anemia or rare tropical disease debate.

After the hip-hop performance, Jonathan hopped in a cab to head to the office while Zara and the baby walked home. She had just settled in for a midmorning breastfeeding session when their apartment door opened unexpectedly.

It was Jonathan.

"Did you forget your phone?" Zara asked.

"No," Jonathan responded, still standing in the doorway. "I have leukemia."

He said the words. She heard the words. And then they hung in the air, unprocessed.

"The doctor called. On my way to work. Told me to turn around. I have to go to New York Presbyterian. Now. I have cancer."

With every sentence, Zara watched Jonathan begin to break down.

The next few hours were crisis management; Zara found child-care and then she and Jonathan headed to the hospital—taking the long way through Central Park for perhaps one more hour of normal. And while, yes, there were people running, people walking with friends, people effortlessly enjoying their day—for Jonathan and Zara, there was nothing normal about it. Life, they suspected, would be forever different.

They weren't wrong. Upon arriving at the hospital it was clear this was life and death. There were meetings and discussions and plans—all of which were simultaneously both calmly methodical and wildly chaotic. At some point in that first terrifying day, Zara found herself back in her own bathroom.

As any mother of small children knows, the bathroom is your best bet at a moment to yourself. It's not guaranteed (what in life is?), but there's something about turning or pushing the lock on a bathroom door that inspires an automatic sigh of relief. The respite is always temporary, which makes it even more sacred.

It was there, on the other side of a locked bathroom door, that Zara stood, alone for the first time, gripping the cool ceramic surface of the bathroom sink to steady herself. She raised her eyes and met her own gaze in the oversized bathroom mirror and considered her story.

What her life would be like as a widowed mother of three.

What life would be like without Jonathan, whom she loved so dearly (especially now, knowing it was *cancer* that was making him so tired and not that he was a sorry excuse of a husband and father).

What she would say at his eulogy.

"I know, it's weird. It's dark. It's twisted," she said as she told me the story. "But I had to go all the way there . . . and then . . . well . . ."

She decided, at least through the process of the treatment, to never go there again.

"That is *not* our story."

MIND. BODY. STORY.

There is one thing I want to make abundantly clear: when it comes to health (when it comes to all things, actually), there are some things that are simply out of your control. It would be irresponsible to suggest that Zara's husband in some way *asked* for cancer.

It is also irresponsible to suggest one can be fully "healed" by mindset. Jonathan needed the aggressive, gruesome, fully Westernized treatment he received, and Zara assured me there was no shortage of highly technical, top-notch chemo poison flowing through his veins.

What we are talking about here, in this chapter, are the things that *are* within your span of control, and one of those things is certainly your mindset.

Zara was living, in real time, the quote often attributed to Jim Rohn that people haphazardly post on social media and is printed on cat posters hanging in dentist offices across the country: "It is the set of the sails, not the direction of the wind that will determine where we will go."

The wind was the reality of the diagnosis, and the sail was her approach to the diagnosis. One you can't control and one you definitely can. And when it comes to your health and the things you can control, you definitely *should*.

Where the Mind Goes, the Body Follows

In the months leading up to the pandemic, I was constantly traveling.

As I mentioned in the previous chapter, the first few weeks of 2020, I was gone more than I was home. During one of my trips, I did one of those "Ask me anything" posts on Instagram stories, and one of the questions was: "How do you travel so much without getting sick? I get sick every time I travel."

I was not able to answer that question in the true spirit in which it was asked because, of course, just a few days later, we found ourselves in a worldwide pandemic where both travel and getting sick took on entirely new meanings.

Pandemic aside, however, that question is not just about health for me. It's about self-storytelling.

I actively *do not* tell myself that I get sick when I travel. I don't have the *luxury* of that story. Let's follow the logic of that story in my life all the way through—like a math equation:

If I told myself I got sick every time I traveled →
And all of my work required travel →
I would be sick every time I worked.

Either that or I would quit my job. The "travel-equals-illness" story is not a story that serves me, so I don't tell it. I never consider it. That story is not allowed anywhere near me.

Now, do I have a set of behaviors and hacks designed to keep me *healthy* while traveling? Absolutely. I buy a liter of water the second I walk through security and fill it up again once I arrive at my destination. I never get on a plane without Emergen-C, and I take it every morning I'm away. I am aware of my sleep—I focus on hours of sleep vs. the time I go to bed because time zones can be a beast to manage. I limit alcohol. I eat food that doesn't bog me down. I try to get outside and go for a walk. During and after the pandemic, I added wearing a mask on the flight and plenty of hand sanitizer.

My behaviors set me up for health, but the story I tell myself ensures it, within the limits of what I can control.

The Self-Care Conundrum

Of course, physical health is only one piece of the puzzle. I was conversing with Amy Morin, author of the runaway bestseller

13 Things Mentally Strong People Don't Do, about the concept of self-care and how it leads to mental toughness. I shared with her that when I hear self-care, I think bubble baths and manicures. We both laughed when we realized we share the same feeling about sitting in a vat of water in our own filth—bubble baths are a *no* for me, and manicures stress me out.

She recommended doing something *you* think is fun, without judgment or wondering if it counts.

I thought about one of the women from the research group, whose mental health was in serious jeopardy. She knew she had to take some time for herself, but it had been so long since she'd done something just for the fun of it, she didn't even know where to start. Of course, that just added anxiety to the issue and stoked the negative story fire. Then, in one of our last sessions, she mentioned she had spent three hours shoveling snow off the roof of her shed-turned-office.

"Did you enjoy it?" I asked her.

She looked at me strangely. "Did I *enjoy* shoveling snow off the roof?" Then she thought about it. Yes, she supposed, she *did* enjoy it. It was hard work, but it was equally Zen. No one bothered her. No one needed something from her when she was shoveling the roof. Or if they did, they couldn't reach her. She was disconnected, outdoors, and feeling meditative.

"Wait a minute!" I said. "You just engaged in some pretty epic self-care."

We often have stories about what "counts" when it comes to our mental health. But what if, instead of worrying about the *right* way to do it, tell yourself the stories of the times you've *gotten it right*. For example, I *love* building Lego sets, but I thought it was a kid thing to do. Then I started buying sets for myself whenever I bought one for the kids. During the many years of travel and stress with work, we would build Legos together all weekend long. Of course, the ability to *buy* a Lego set is a privilege not everyone is afforded; those things cost a small fortune. And during the pandemic when our finances were unstable, the Lego-budget didn't make the cut. In 2021, business had picked up, but the Legos hadn't. I found myself stressed and unable to have fun or engage in self-care. And then I was reminded of the Lego weekend stories and got back to building.

You can't scroll through social media without seeing some quote or video or influencer talking about how important self-care is. That's a lot of stress and pressure on something that's supposed to alleviate stress and pressure. You can eliminate a lot of that by deciding what *your* version of self-care is. So far, I have yet to see a guru telling adults to play with Legos, but that's what works for *me*.

Remember: your self-care story is yours alone to write and tell.

If there are changes you'd like to make in your health, whether related to illness, weight, or mental well-being, here's some good news: nine chapters in, you now know exactly how. The same method that works for your business and career challenges will work for you when it comes to your health. Four simple steps can change everything. Catch your stories in the act, analyze them to better understand where they came from and why they're there, choose better stories, and install them as your automated operating system.

Let's start by taking a look at all the different ways our stories show themselves.

STEP ONE: CATCH YOUR STORIES AT WORK

Meet Cori.

The moment my video call with Cori connects, the screen reveals a face that you can't help but smile back at. Cori seems perpetually cheerful and quick to laugh. She works as a corporate trainer, spending a lot of time in front of groups, and it's easy to see how she shines in her role.

Now, however, Cori's on the other side—she's a participant in *my* group and focused on addressing the stories she tells herself and how they might be working against her in terms of her health and, in particular, her weight.

"During the pandemic," she says, "I'm not moving as much. I've been working from home. We just aren't doing the things we used to, and we're probably eating not as great as we used to. I was like, oh wow, the scale is really creeping up."

I raise my hand. Been there. *Am* there.

She smiles even more broadly. "I was, like, it's fine, I'd rather be a little bit chubby, you know, than forgo all the yummy things in life." As she says it, a thought crosses her mind like a cloud crossing the path of the sun. Then, as if seeing the shadow, she continues.

"I think that's an excuse I tell myself versus trying to be more in control of what's going into my mouth." She laughs a little. I laugh a little back in recognition. Recognition of a story that sounds all too familiar often makes people laugh a little.

And so I ask Cori, simply, "How do you feel?"

For the first time since we'd spoken, the smile leaves her face.

"Not great," she says.

If you are someone who has struggled with your weight, let me pause here for a moment and say: do not let the importance of this admission be lost on you. There is so much good about the body positivity movement, namely that bodies of all different shapes and sizes are worthy of love. And while this collective shift in understanding is valid and important, it does *not* invalidate your personal feelings about *your body*. If you *love* your body as it is, great! If you've separated society's body ideals and pressures from your own physical being and, after doing so, you still don't feel your best in your body as it is now, that's okay too!

In fact, if "not great" is how you feel about *any* area of your health and well-being, that's reason enough to take out the binoculars and start scanning the surface for a glimpse of story masses that live just outside your scope of conscious awareness.

Keep in mind that these statements are as varied as the people who believe them. These statements can include but are not limited to:

- I always get sick when I travel.
- I am just a low-energy person.
- I could never run a mile.
- I am just big-boned.
- If there's a flu going around, I'll catch it.
- I just don't have time for myself.
- I'll sleep when I'm dead.

I task Cori the goal of digging a little deeper for her statements. When she returns a week later, she's armed with a few key ones that she realizes have been consistent companions—phrases like *I'll always struggle with this* and *I love myself, I love my body.*

Read those two again:

- I will always struggle with this.
- I love myself and my body.

Notice something strange? How can these two contradictory statements exist in the same space? Here's where self-storytelling and health can be challenging—our health stories aren't always what they seem. Over time, the iceberg of our hidden stories builds up in layers, but that doesn't mean that all the layers *agree.* Stories can contradict. They can seem to be polar opposites. They can point us in different directions or drive us in circles.

Faced with conflicting stories, it can be hard to know which ones to believe. Breaking through them takes work, but it's work that needs to be done to cross the gap.

Cori, however, recognizes that the second phrase might be a "well-dressed excuse."

"I love myself," she says, with a laugh. "I can drink all the wine and eat all the cake."

Keep an eye out for these statements that appear to be positive but actually keep you further from where you want to go.

STEP TWO: ANALYZE YOUR SELF-STORIES

"This was the most impactful piece for me," Cori confessed during one of our conversations. "I mean, I can't believe the stories in my iceberg. I thought all the way back to when I was a child and remembered comparing my legs to my cousin's legs and even as a *child* noticing how different our legs looked, how skinny hers were, and how that small story, that I can remember as clear as day, has impacted how I behave as an adult."

The level of detail Cori could recall was also shocking. "I remember, when we were older, being at that same cousin's cabin and going out to a bar that has these amazing nachos. And I was like, 'We should order the nachos!' And skinny beautiful cousin said, 'Yeah, I'm kind of like just watching what I eat.' And I thought to myself, *She weighs like five pounds, and she's watching what she eats?* And then I wondered if I should watch what *I* eat. So, instead of ordering the beer that I wanted, I ended up ordering like some sad vodka soda cocktail."

She had bigger stories in there, too—stories about her father. "My sister and I have both struggled for as long as I can remember. Our dad was really unhealthy. He had a gastric bypass, had diabetes, had heart failure, and ended up ultimately passing away a couple of years ago. My mom never had any issues." She smiles slightly as she glances upward in feigned exasperation and says for effect, "Why did we get those genes?!"

It's amazing the things you can uncover about yourself by asking a simple set of questions. If the old adage is true that knowing is half the battle, a few minutes of analysis alone can make the gap easier to cross.

Ask: Is this true?

Whenever I traveled, I would feel extremely anxious about the amount of sleep I was getting. Sleep is a key pillar of health, and I had always been told growing up that I needed a lot of it. If I wasn't feeling well after sleeping over at a friend's house, "Well, you need a lot of sleep," my mother would say. If I got sick the first day of spring break in college after pulling an all-nighter for a test, "Well, you need a lot of sleep," my mother would say.

Behind the statement were a few of the stories of when I really *did* get sick as a kid, though I can't imagine sleep was always the cause (I was a pretty lousy hand-washer, too). Underneath all of them was the theme that I needed *more* sleep than the people around me.

That statement and the stories propping it up haunted me late into my adulthood until I had children. If you've ever had a newborn in your home (heck, even a puppy), you know that sleep is hard to come by. And *yet,* I managed to survive. The girl who couldn't survive without sleep became a mother of two-under-two—and survived. Clearly, there was a story there that needed to be analyzed.

One of the questions I encouraged you to ask during Step Two of the process was, "Is this true?"

I didn't know the answer. *Did* I need a lot of sleep? How much is a lot? I decided to put it to the test. Over the course of several months and then over a year, I determined how much sleep I actually *do* need. It turns out that seven hours is my sweet spot. Eight hours is great but unnecessary on a daily basis. At six, I am functional, but it's not ideal.

There you go. I spent decades believing a story that preoccupied me and changed my behavior. And it was a story that was handed to me—one that I took without even once considering whether or not it was true. Understanding it better meant freedom from the subtle fear of it.

Own It

Seth was a young, handsome guy grinding out the hustle in New York City. Whether it was the stress or the times, Seth had picked up a smoking habit. Multiple times a day, he'd step out of his midtown office and grab a smoke on the street. He'd smoke in bars and at bus stops. He'd smoke socially and alone.

And he hated it. He tried quitting almost as soon as he started and then every day after and was never able to gain any traction. He would often complain to his roommate—a gentleman some twenty years his senior whom he'd found via an ad in the paper—until finally, annoyed with Seth's constant lamenting about wanting to quit, the roommate said, "Do you, though? Do you want to quit? It seems to me you quite enjoy smoking. Maybe you should just embrace it? *Be* a smoker. Own it. Maybe that will help."

Seth had never considered that. What if he fully embraced being a smoker? Maybe that wouldn't be so bad. The next day, every time he lit up, he said to himself, "Look at me! I'm a smoker! I *like* smoking!" But by the end of the night, he had a really bad taste in his mouth, and it wasn't from the tar and nicotine concoction.

"Smoking is gross," he said to his roommate. "I actually loathe smoking."

And he quit.

Sometimes fully owning a story is the only way to truly see it for what it is and then be able to let it go.

STEP THREE: CHOOSE A STORY THAT SERVES YOU

"That is *not* our story."

With those words, Zara had made a storytelling choice—though she probably didn't call it that at the time. Understanding that they were engaging in the fight of a lifetime, understanding that she couldn't possibly understand how dark the days would get, understanding how fragile both her spirit and Jonathan's could become,

Zara decided that throughout Jonathan's treatment, she would fiercely guard the stories they told themselves. No entertaining "worst-case scenarios." No losing themselves down any "what if" rabbit holes. She wanted no story or reference to know whether Jonathan had a 1 percent chance or 99 percent chance of survival. And while some may call it denial, for Zara, it was strategy. Because not only did Zara choose *not* to engage in the bad stories, she chose to *believe* any possible good ones.

"I'll never forget the conversation with Jonathan's doctor," Zara said. Right from the beginning, the doctors communicated almost exclusively with Zara. Jonathan only wanted to focus on the treatment at hand, one step at a time. His job would be to fight for his life; Zara's job was to give him the motivation and information to swing the odds of that fight in his favor. The doctor, one of the best in the country, looked at Zara and said with complete confidence and zero fanfare, "I know what he's got; I know I can cure it." The doctor warned Zara it was going to be aggressive. Essentially, they were going to take everything out of Jonathan—all the cells, the bad *and* the good. He would be admitted into the hospital and not be allowed out for a month.

"She told me to see it as a rebirth. And I liked that story. I decided to fully embrace that story. To celebrate it, even. What a beautiful thing to be completely new in your forties. Few people get that chance." Zara told Jonathan the rebirth story and shared the doctor's recommendation to lean into the idea. "Those who resist that story," Zara said, "have a harder time and less desirable results." If Jonathan could surrender and embrace that story, too, the mind could help lead the body down the path of healing.

To be clear, Zara reiterated the seriousness: "Make no mistake. This was not a woo-woo approach." One of the most technical hospitals in the country was pumping her husband full of the most highly advanced medicine that science could create. But even so, choosing a story of hope, choosing to lean into the story of rebirth instead of complete and utter cellular destruction, was an important piece of the treatment.

Zara's story choice was one of life and death; I hope with everything within me that your self-stories never have to endure that kind of pressure. But I also hope you know it doesn't take a life-and-death situation for your self-stories to matter.

A Lesson in Time Bending and Community Creating

Meet Michelle.

Michelle has no time. She has a big, full-time job. She has kids who, like most kids, require a lot of her time and energy. And, to add to it, she and her family have been through the wringer when it comes to health issues. After her husband's diagnosis of Crohn's disease, followed by Michelle's own diagnosis of Lynch syndrome and followed by another terrifying diagnosis for her husband, kidney cancer, it seemed as if the cards were never stacked in Michelle's favor.

Michelle had a whole library of stories she could, and did, tell herself about all the reasons she didn't have time to work out and why she was too tired to exercise. And she could add to that library the story of how, at the time of our interview, the group fitness events she had once loved were no longer an option.

But Michelle wanted *change*. And she had come to the conclusion that no change would stick if she didn't first change the stories she was telling herself. So she went searching for stories that served her—namely, stories about time and creating community. She found the story of the day when she dropped her daughter off at an activity and then went back to her car to call her mother while she waited for her daughter's practice to be done—but then realized that there was an empty track right in front of her. "Why not walk around the track *while* I talk to my mother?" she thought. And so, she did. It was just one time but remembering that story in full detail inspired Michelle. Instead of, "I don't have any time," her story became, "I am really good at making time."

Additionally, Michelle found a new part of her group fitness story she had forgotten. Yes, she loved going to work out with her friends, but she was the one who got them all there in the first place. "I was the one encouraging people to come join me. I got a whole group of my friends to start going!" It wasn't *just* that Michelle enjoyed group fitness. Michelle was great at inspiring people to *join* her in group fitness.

Armed with these two chosen stories, Michelle felt lighter and more hopeful. She reached out to a few of her friends and family and, though they couldn't physically be together, they all happened to have treadmills in their homes. They would meet every day after work, get on a group call, and walk independently together.

When one of Michelle's walking partners got sick and couldn't walk anymore, Michelle, to her surprise, kept going. "That's not something I would have done before. I would have let it slip," Michelle confessed. But her stories kept her going.

This shift was no small thing for Michelle. During our final session, as we struggled to say goodbye (it turns out talking with someone about their innermost stories creates a deep bond), Michelle looked at me from the desk in her home office and said, "All I can say is this has unlocked this piece of me that wasn't alive for a very long time . . . and because everybody's been sick and we've had our challenges, it's like I just closed that off for five years." Michelle paused as she regained her composure. "It's just made a difference so fast . . . Everyone around me can see that difference already. I can't afford *not* to do this."

Michelle can no longer afford to tell herself stories that don't serve her.

And neither can you.

Losing Sleep or Gaining Time

I have a friend who struggles with sleep. She can *get* to sleep fine, and she's also good at *staying* asleep throughout the night. Her problem, actually, isn't sleep at all; it's waking up. Every morning she jolts awake at 3:30 or 4:00 a.m. and can't go back to sleep. She'll lie in bed for hours, in pitch darkness, holding her eyes closed, willing her mind to silence the sudden, unwanted chatter—and then begrudgingly get up to face the day at 6:00 or 7:00 a.m.

It was extremely disturbing to her. She was literally losing sleep over—well, losing sleep.

Having been through my own sleep story, I asked my friend if she was tired throughout the day. "No," she said. "Not excessively so. I just get up so early."

I shared a story with her that I had recently heard when I was interviewing Ryan Serhant of *Million Dollar Listing New York*. While the rest of us walk around in a world that has twenty-four hours in a day, Ryan seems to have forty. And while I sat wondering how it was physically possible, he revealed a clue. "I wake up every morning at 4:00 a.m.," he told me.

Whoa. No matter what time of year or what point of daylight savings torture you're in, it is definitely *dark* at 4:00 a.m., and as my friend lamented, there is something that just feels wrong about waking up when it's dark.

"What do you do at that hour?!" I asked Ryan. It turns out he sends emails. He had tried having someone else send emails on his behalf the way any productivity expert or coach might suggest. But for Ryan, emails were essential and, as he learned the hard way, not outsourceable. "So, I wake up, answer emails, work out . . . and that's how I start my day."

"See?" I said to my friend after telling her the story. "You are waking up at the same time as a man who credits some of his success to waking up early—and you don't even have to try! I'm actually jealous of your early mornings." She smiled at me. "I never thought of it that way."

From then on, my friend chose to tell herself the story of the other successful people in the world who wake before the sun rises. She sees her early mornings as an advantage instead of a flaw, and it's been sweet dreams ever since.

STEP FOUR: INSTALL YOUR CHOSEN STORIES

Back to Cori. An A+ member of my research group, Cori showed up all the way every time—although she admitted to being a little skeptical at first. "Honestly"—she hesitated a second—"I will say, I started out, and I was like, I don't know how helpful this is going to be." Cori's skepticism was well intentioned. She had the knowledge to change—she knew, *logically,* what to do—and she also had the drive. "I just didn't have the accountability," she said.

It turned out that starting each day with her stories helped. The stories Cori told herself included fan favorites like, "I hate the gym." But in the dead of winter, with few other options, that statement wasn't serving her. Instead, Cori worked to uncover a story that would. She found two. "There was this one time where I had the most incredible run on a treadmill and another time when I had a really awesome time running around the indoor track."

It may sound crazy but retelling herself those two simple stories each morning motivated her to get up and go to the gym. And, in fact, it went *beyond* Cori. "This was the real epiphany," she told me. "This is when I knew this storytelling thing really works." That holiday break, instead of just sitting around their house, not moving, Cori, her husband, *and* her kids got up and went to the gym. "We *never* would have done that otherwise," she said. "We went to the gym three times as a family that whole week. The kids ran with me or played basketball; my husband worked out in the weights area. It created some cool memories, and we discovered a whole different way to spend time together as a family."

Cori came back to her diligence of starting each day with those stories—and the new ones she discovered in the process. "Waking up each morning and telling myself these stories," she said, "that gave me the accountability I needed, the motivation . . . I think I actually have a higher amount of trust in myself after going through this self-storytelling process."

If you've struggled to achieve a health goal even when you have everything it takes and know what to do, a complete lack of trust *in yourself* is likely what's missing. Saying you'll show up and then not doing it over and over and over takes its toll on any relationship, including the one you have with *you*. Start by showing up every morning to tell yourself the stories—that will inspire the behavior that creates the results you want and deserve.

Be Trigger-Ready

When it comes to health and fitness goals, triggers are lurking everywhere—behind the time of day, the fridge door, your mood, the weather, and that commercial about a Snickers bar that makes you raid your children's Halloween candy. They happen in a split second, but their impact, especially compounded over days, months, or a lifetime, adds up. A lifetime of skipping a morning workout versus a lifetime of getting up the first time the alarm sounds will create very different results. Having stories ready for these trigger moments can change your life, no matter what or how random your triggers may be.

Ironically, one of my triggers is Michael exercising.

I realized it one Sunday morning when Michael walked into the living room with his workout clothes on, laced up his shoes, and left the house to go for a run.

And I was *super* annoyed. Because he made it look so easy. He didn't walk around for an hour avoiding it, he didn't think about going for half the morning and then decide not to, he didn't make excuses for all the reasons he shouldn't go. He just *went*.

I knew he hadn't actually done anything wrong, and, in fact, he was showing me how to do it right. After my irrational irritation settled, I realized Michael getting his weekend workout in before me has been a longtime trigger. When he effortlessly walks out the door, a rapid sequence of "I don't have enough time" stories and "I have to take care of the kids" stories and "*someone* needs to do the laundry" stories flashes before my eyes, kicking off a spiral that inevitably leads to another skipped workout.

On that particular Sunday morning, after recognizing the trigger for what it was, I decided to insert some of my chosen stories in an effort to stop the spiral and regain control.

- I told myself the story of dancing the night away at a wedding a few years ago (yes, that hypothetical situation in chapter 7 was me)—I'd been working out and eating well and felt so beautiful and strong.
- I told myself the story of a night the spring after my daughter was born—we had gone to a charity event, and I was wearing an amazing dress and felt so strong and vibrant.
- I told myself the story of a compliment a friend had given me just the fall prior after I had recommitted to regular exercise and how proud I was of myself.

I told myself a few more of *these* kinds of stories, and within ninety seconds, I had my spin shoes on, eager to get on my bike to ride. I told the kids to read or watch a movie or play video games; I didn't care—I was going to exercise!

One hour, five hundred calories, and an envious look from Michael later (because my spin session was way more fun than his run), I felt like a new person.

Action in the right direction can be tough, especially if your life feels a bit like a minefield of triggers to throw you off course. In those moments, have your chosen stories ready—stories to remind you where you want to go and why.

HEALTHILY EVER AFTER

Jonathan remained in the hospital for a month straight, a steady flow of chemo pumping into his body every hour of every day. The treatment was so aggressive they gave Jonathan the freedom to self-administer morphine as he needed.

The treatment ravaged his body to the point that he couldn't even swallow his own saliva. Zara would arrive every morning to find her husband lying on his side, his mouth slightly open, allowing the saliva to slowly drip out onto his pillow. For six hours, she would sit with him. She would consult with physicians, careful to never do so within earshot of Jonathan, and report back to him how well the treatment was working—even if there had been a setback—because no one could expect rebirth to be easy. She would then leave the hospital and head home to spend the rest of the evening with their children.

"Every day, I walked," Zara said. It was about two miles, nothing for a New Yorker, but as Zara recalled the commute, something occurred to her. "Every day, I stepped out of the hospital, pulled out my phone, and called one of a handful of friends. For the whole walk home, I told them the story of the day . . . not what went wrong, but about how well Jonathan was doing. How the treatment was working. What the next steps and milestones were. My friends just . . . listened. They let me tell the whole story, and at the end of it, they would say, 'Zara, Jonathan's doing so great! You've got this. You've both got this.' After hours and hours in the hospital—a completely exhausting environment—telling them the story of the day energized me.

"And as I walked in the front door, and my two oldest ran to me, and I picked the baby up into my arms, I could smile and say without any shadows of doubt, 'Daddy is doing so good! It's working!

Daddy is getting better and will be home with us soon!'" She paused. "As if I spoke that story into existence . . . every day . . . on my walk home."

There were two things I took away from this part of Zara's story. First, the undeniable power of a story spoken out loud. How you really can speak a story and create a reality. Second, perhaps more importantly, what a blessing it is to have people in life who will *listen* to our stories and how we can *be* that person for someone else. I think about the friends who, I'm sure, had busy lives of their own, yet picked up the phone and, for two miles, gave Zara the space to tell her stories. We should all strive to be that friend.

As for Jonathan, I am thrilled to report that he did take well to the treatment. After the initial month in the hospital plus ten days to regain strength, Jonathan's treatment shifted to five months of one week in the hospital for chemo, three weeks at home followed by years of tapered bloodwork and doctor visits. His cancer is now in remission.

Zara first told me Jonathan's story as a friend during a stroll through the park on the far east side of Manhattan. When, a year later, I asked if I might share their story in this book, she suggested I speak with Jonathan, too—to hear his version, his story. Jonathan's account, while not incongruent, was different from Zara's—a difference you would expect coming from the person who endured the treatment. However, the commitment to the stories he told himself was the same. In fact, there was one moment that, unknown to either of them, was identical.

After receiving the call in the cab that Friday morning in February and then heading to the hospital to what was ahead, the doctor told Jonathan and Zara to take the weekend. Take it to process. Take it to enjoy what was left of the "normal" they knew. Treatment would start next week.

That Monday morning, Jonathan rose early, kissed his kids and his wife as they left for school drop-off and headed to the bathroom to take a shower. There was something about turning the lock on that bathroom door—how it created a space of temporary respite. A moment alone with his thoughts. It was there—the water in the shower running, the steam slowly crowding the edges of the over-sized bathroom mirror—that Jonathan gripped the cool ceramic surface of the bathroom sink and steadied himself. He raised his eyes and met his own gaze reflected in the glass.

"You gotta do this."

And so the story began.

10

MONEY AND FINANCES

Stories Don't Grow on Trees . . .

Money stories are passed down through families.
That's the story I need to break.

— A M Y

Imagine you lend a friend $100.

Or maybe you're not even lending her the money. Maybe there's a group of you out for happy hour, and to make things easy, you pick up the tab, and everyone's going to pay you back. You don't even think twice about it—you know your friends are good for it, and you secretly love accruing points on your card anyway. (Cabo, here you come!)

Everyone pays you back fairly promptly. That's the nature of this particular group of friends. Some send you the money digitally before you reach the front door; some take a week or two because they're gonna hand you a stack of bills. This doesn't bother you either—when was the last time you had actual dollar bills in your wallet? Worth the wait.

And then, on a Wednesday afternoon as you're standing at school pickup, the last friend to pay strolls up. Amidst the chaos of school dismissal, she hands you what looks a *little* like a $100 bill.

But only a little.

It's got Benjamin Franklin on it, but it's Benjamin Franklin if he were drawn by a second-grader. The green is admittedly brighter than that of a standard bill, as if painted with watercolor. The "100" in the corner is written in Sharpie—not even the fine-tip kind—and the whole back side is white. Just a regular old piece of paper.

"Thanks for the other night," your friend says.

You look down at the scrap of paper in your hand. "Is this a . . ." you trail off. "This is a joke, isn't it?"

I mean, what else could it be if not a not-that-funny joke?

Your friend assures you she's not joking. "Money," she says, "is just a belief system. If we all *believe* this is $100, then it *is* $100." She smiles brightly, takes the hand of her child, who is shouting something about going over to Caleb's house, and walks off, leaving you holding the worthless scrap of paper in your hand.

Here's the thing: your friend's not entirely wrong.

She's not entirely right, of course—that scrap of construction paper really is worthless.

But she's not wrong about the *concept*.

Money is the ultimate story.

In fact, the only reason money *exists* is because of the power of story. The cash in your wallet, the numbers on your banking app—they're simply a belief system based on a story that money has value. We've all chosen to believe that a dollar, a franc, a peso, a pound, or a yuan have a trusted value, and that allows us to use them as a medium of exchange.

That shared belief in the value of money is one of the oldest, most powerful, and arguably most important stories in human history. It allowed the development of the earliest economies. It meant we could trade goods over long distances. And it's the reason you don't have to carve shavings off a block of gold to buy groceries, or trade wheat or apples with your plumber to get your dishwasher fixed.

But money isn't just the ultimate story. It's also the most heavily *loaded* story.

Perhaps you've heard that "money doesn't grow on trees," or that "money is the root of all evil," or that "a light purse is a heavy curse." Maybe you, yourself, have warned your insistent teenager through clenched teeth that you, in fact, are *not* made of money or that "all that glitters is not gold." Maybe you've seen an acquaintance post a photo on a tarmac, their right foot placed precariously on the first step of an airstair leading to the cabin of a private jet, and thought to yourself, "Rich people are greedy."

Regardless of the words you use, by now you can see these sentences for what they are: iceberg statements pointing to the enormous, hidden money story beneath the surface of our awareness. And those examples are only the *universal* statements. The personalized versions are far more varied and even more powerful:

- "I am bad with money."
- "I'll never be rich."
- "I can't afford nice things."
- "Money is scarce."
- "Money's not my thing."
- "I like to live for the moment, not save for a rainy day."
- "I need a job with a steady paycheck."
- "I always struggle to pay my bills."

And, as if in recognition of the overpopulation of money stories allowed to run rampant and feast on the fruit of whatever gardens we might attempt to grow, so are there an ample number of texts designed to redefine wealth and money: *The Total Money Makeover*, *Rich Dad Poor Dad*, *You Are a Badass at Making Money*, *The Law of Divine Compensation*, and *Think and Grow Rich*, to name a few. And, of course, there are the classics like *The Science of Getting Rich*.

(I would have loved to have seen the look on my son's fourth-grade teacher's face when, after being assigned to read a nonfiction book and realizing that we were fresh out of age-appropriate texts in our house, my son read the first few chapters of *The Science of Getting Rich*. "I didn't understand a lot of what they were saying, Mama. But chapter one *did* talk about everyone has the right to be rich.")

Books. Proverbs. Quotes. Pithy statements and self-monologues. When it comes to money stories, there is no shortage. And each is entirely unique and extremely complex. Every individual's money stories are shaped by many factors including, but not limited to, our community, family makeup, and race. For example, I am a white woman born into a middle-class family. This reality means my money stories are likely very different from someone whose [insert gender, insert race, insert cultural expectations, insert the income bracket you were born into, the list goes on . . .] is different from mine.

No, not all money stories begin as equal, but one thing they *do* share is that they, like most self-stories, often remain undetected and allowed to run rampant through our lives.

THE MONEY VOICE INSIDE

This hidden money story—this giant iceberg of beliefs—is the very thing one of the participants was trying to come to grips with when I met with her.

Meet Amy.

A late-forties, almost fiftysomething woman from Texas, Amy is smart and introspective. She has achieved great things in her life, including running a massively successful entrepreneurial endeavor and holding a top-level leadership role in a corporate education environment, both of which require superior leadership and communication skills. She has also overcome several significant obstacles, including failed relationships that threatened her self-worth and livelihood. In short, Amy is a badass.

It's no surprise, then, that when Amy comes to me, she has a very clear idea of the problem she is facing: the voice in her head that simply wouldn't shut up about money.

"I have a tape going through my head of stories," she says. "Now that I work for myself, I don't have that steady paycheck coming in. I'm always anxious about money."

If, like Amy, you've ever been anxious about money—or if you're *always* anxious about money—first, take a breath. You are very, very un-alone. Second, it's time to walk through the self-storytelling steps because the greatest ghostwriter that ever lived exists inside you and is posting daily content about how rich you should or should not be.

STEP ONE: CATCH YOUR STORIES AT WORK

It's clear that I don't have to teach Amy the power of story. But knowing there's a story isn't the same as being able to catch it in midflight. Amy has no trouble embracing the idea that her stories are holding her back, but she's stalled on where to go next.

Yes, she's got stories running through her head, but I urge her to get more specific. Her first task is to identify the story—to find the clues that might help her catch the story in action and get more specific than a general sense of lack or anxiety about money.

When she appears for our next one-on-one session, she's found the obvious ones.

"I'm bad with money," she says, reading from her list. "I never have enough money. Where's the next client coming from?"

She goes on to tell me more details about how those iceberg statements are triggered. She would love to do more fun things with her family, like take a ski vacation or go to the beach. But each time she thinks about planning a holiday, the voice in her head speaks about how much it will cost and how she can't afford it. And if she happens to see other people in her own social circle taking a trip, she can't help but ask herself how *they* can take such amazing vacations but she can't. "How much does all of that cost?" she wonders. But instead of trying to figure it out—instead of actually investigating to see if perhaps she and her family *could* afford a tropical vacation—she won't even allow herself to consider it. "I can't even allow myself to go down that path," she says.

Instead, she stays stuck in her "I will never have enough money" story rut.

True or false (remember, the brain doesn't often distinguish the two), Amy's money story was a) keeping her from enjoying the money she *did* have and b) was keeping her from making *more* money. Her story had become a self-fulfilling prophecy.

Amy suspected this. She could see that her story of not having enough money was the root cause of, well, not having enough money. And she wasn't wrong. Just as money is a story, so is it an energy. If you have your resistance up, the money energy cannot flow freely. Your story creates a blockage. Remove the story, and you remove the blockage, allowing the money to flow freely and at will.

To remove the story, however, it was important to first explore what lay beneath the surface of the water. What stories from Amy's past were propping up this belief about her current reality and future?

STEP TWO: ANALYZE YOUR SELF-STORIES

What's strange—at least to Amy—about her money story is that she grew up in an affluent family. "We've never been without," she says, "and we've always had nice things. But there was an undertone of 'we don't have enough money.'"

This incongruence seems to jar something in Amy, and more mixed messages begin to emerge. She recalls her stepdad commenting, "I guess we'll have to eat beans for a while."

"We never had to eat beans," she says, incredulous. "They had no idea what it actually meant."

But that contradiction has settled into Amy over the years. Growing up in abundance, but with messages of scarcity, has left Amy with money anxieties *even when she has it.*

"You grow up [with these messages]," she says, "you look around, and you have everything you need—which then meant you *didn't* have enough."

Now, however, with a clear grasp of her story and where it came from, it's time to make new choices. That's something Amy is motivated to do as her kids begin to grow into adults with money stories of their own.

Somewhere in her past, there are stories that contradict the one Amy's been telling herself. Those are the stories we need to find.

I ask her, "Is there a time where you really were good with money?" I suggest to her that it must take some financial skill to quit a job and start a company the way she did. Before our next meeting, she agrees to dig in the past for stories of a financially savvy Amy—the one I think she's lost touch with.

THE FOUR MONEY STORIES YOU SHOULD EVALUATE

Most, if not all, of us have anxious moments concerning money. When it comes to analyzing your money story, there are a couple of specific, though not always obvious, places to look. It is the elusive nature of these self-stories that makes them some of the most difficult to uncover. For example, one of the paradoxical things about money stories—something Amy is discovering—is they're *not* tied to how much you actually have. Which means money stories cross every demographic, from the poverty-stricken to the trust-fund endowed.

No matter what our income, we all have some variation on four basic money stories.

1. Your story about how much money you have

I have a friend who is a saver. I don't mean she is able to tuck a little aside for a rainy day. I mean *she has seven figures in a savings account.*

While many people would find a deep sense of financial security in that level of wealth, my friend agonizes over it. She tells herself she should invest it. That inflation is eating away at it. That she's missing out on a chance to grow that wealth in any meaningful way. And so she walks around constantly afraid of money.

For my friend, taking a look at this particular aspect of her money might reveal stories from her childhood—what her parents valued. There are probably some stories in there about liquidity. Some stories in there about using money to make more money. About the "right" way to "do" money. It is highly likely that these stories are so big they keep her frozen in place. Instead of calling a financial advisor or calling a real estate agent who specializes in investment properties, she does nothing, and therefore, nothing changes.

Keep in mind that because money is just a really big story, it is also entirely relative. Someone who secured the first salaried position in their family's history at $25,000 could see their story as just as good or better than the story of somebody who makes $250,000 but whose friends make a million. If you're struggling with money, examining the stories that fuel your understanding of how much you have is an important place to start.

2. Your story about how much money you need

I have another friend who, from the outside, appears to have everything. A beautiful home, a wonderful family, friends. He has a good job, too, though that is where the "perfect life" starts to fall apart a bit. To clarify, it *is* a good job; he makes a good salary and is good at the work he does. But there's a lot about the job he doesn't love— the two biggest things being the small-minded, micromanaging nature of the leadership, and that his talents aren't fully utilized. He feels he has so much capacity that will never be recognized at the company.

My friend has worked there for more than a decade.

The question is, then, why doesn't he leave? Why not apply somewhere else or start something of his own? These are fair questions—questions that he himself has asked. And he has explored other options, but every time he talks with a company that values his big-idea capabilities, it's a start-up with limited funds. He would have to take a pay cut to leave his big corporate job.

The next logical question anyone might ask, one that he certainly has asked himself, is: Would it be worth it? Sure, it's less pay, but it's also less agony and potentially more joy and fulfillment. And if it goes well, couldn't it mean *more* pay at some point? And even if it is less pay, can he afford less money to get more lifestyle? It's a compromise many make, after all.

The answer, for him, is *no*.

Even though the new role would make him wealthy by many, if not most, yardsticks, he *needs* more money. Why?

Because he earns less than his dad.

Now, I am not going to go into the depths of his story with his father. That's not my story to tell, and, to be honest, I'm not entirely sure he realizes it's there. But the thing for you to understand is that it's a money story. The roots of his behavior are buried deep in a story that really has nothing to do with how much money he needs to run his life. It's a story about the money he needs to feel *worthy*.

This is also the money story Amy is digging into—how much is enough? And if you have what you need—then why are you anxious?

3. Your story about where money comes from

I was talking to a man whose work situation was in flux. He was faced with the prospect of having to move to a new city to keep his job. He doesn't want to. He's happy where he is. He has a home, a life.

"But," he says, "I can't leave the job. The money's too good. I'll never make that money anywhere else."

His belief is that the money he's accustomed to can only come from one source: his current job. But where does his money *really* come from? Is it from the company he works for, or does it come from his experience and ability? Is it from outside or inside?

4. Your story about how money should be used

Imagine two people. Their financial situation, for the purpose of this example, is identical. They have the same amount of debt, the same amount of income, the same set of standard expenses. Everything is the same.

Person A decides to hire someone to come and clean their home on a weekly basis. It costs $100 a week. Person A's logic is that this frees up a significant amount of their time that used to be spent on cleaning but can instead now be spent on other things—work, exercise, or free time with the family.

Person B has heard that Person A hired someone to clean their house once a week but has no interest in doing so. Person B is perfectly capable of keeping the house tidy on their own and, in fact, enjoys doing so. Person B would much rather *keep* that $100 than spend it on something they can do for free.

Who is right?

Both people feel they're using their money wisely, and they both think they're saving money, but which one of them is right?

They both are, provided their stories serve them.

This is a big one. This is the one that can come between friends and tear apart marriages. You've likely heard that the number-one thing couples argue about is money, and I'll be honest, it has long been a point of friction in my own household. My husband and I have entirely different beliefs when it comes to how money should be used. These beliefs are built on a lifetime of stories. Our childhoods were, in very general terms, similar; we were both raised in middle-class, two-parent households. Neither were rich, neither were poor; both families were always conscientious about money going in and money going out. Yet Michael's stories make him much more inclined to keep money close, and my stories have propelled me to send money out, like a fisherman casting a line, to see what comes back in. There have been countless occasions, big and small, where the clash of our beliefs in this area has caused tension. It wasn't until we were able to see these beliefs for what they are and understand where they came from that we were able to move forward in ways that served our family best.

The only way to keep these stories from stomping through your life like Godzilla in a fit of fiery destruction is to analyze them. To take a good look below the surface and figure out where the stories come from and why they are there.

Money stories are some of the most difficult to pin down, but you can dig into them with the same questions you use to analyze any story:

- Where did this story come from?
- Is this story true?
- Why is the story there?
- What price do I pay for this story?
- Does this story serve me?
- Where am I in this story?

When it comes to money stories, it's important to approach this part of the process with a sense of curiosity rather than from a place of judgment. Seek to understand. There's no "right" money story. There are only *stories*—some of which serve you and some of which don't.

STEP THREE: CHOOSE A STORY THAT SERVES YOU

"After the big revelation from our last call . . . that money stories are handed down through families," Amy said in the first few minutes of our third session, "I started looking for good stories to replace those old ones . . . [but] I feel like I'm struggling a bit in finding the stories that are specific about money."

First of all, Amy is an excellent student of this method. After analyzing the stories she tells herself about money and determining where those stories came from, she immediately moved to the next step, which was to find and then choose better stories to replace the ones that weren't serving her—an endeavor that proved to be more challenging than she expected.

I wasn't surprised. When you've been telling yourself certain stories for a lifetime—in Amy's case, stories about money—it can take more than a revelation to fill the story-void you create by putting the old stories on the shelf. Be patient.

Patient and also open to seeing stories in a different light.

Tilt the Prism

I mentioned earlier that, in our home, I am known as the spender. I'm the one who plays "fast and loose" with money. And don't get me wrong, there are plenty of true stories in my past where I flat-out failed at money.

The time I rented an apartment and needed to keep a second job to afford it.

The time I had a boyfriend in Minnesota when I had moved to New Mexico, and I bought plane tickets to see him every other weekend even though I was a broke grad student with tens of thousands of dollars in student loans.

Or! Speaking of loans, the time I applied for financial aid and then used it all to go shopping.

Or the time (okay, the two times), I purchased a car, and the only way I could afford it was with financing over six years.

I fought with Netflix back when they sent DVDs, insisting that I canceled my membership *before* my monthly billing was due, and could they please refund the $7 because my bank account was overdrawn. Even in high school, I had this habit of tucking my cash in the fold of my sock. The number of times I stood at the concession stand at the football game and was unable to buy the popcorn I had ordered because my money fell out of my sock.

Yes, I have done some no-way-around-it dumb things with money.

However, I have also made some financial decisions that, if you looked at them one way, may have appeared irresponsible; but if you tilt the story ever so slightly on its side, it casts a different colored light altogether.

About a week after Michael and I bought our first home together, I was at a girlfriend's house for happy hour, and she mentioned the house across the street from her in a super desirable neighborhood was about to go up for sale. Michael had been talking for years about doing more real estate investing, and this sounded like the perfect house. The girls and I walked over, looked in the windows. I tried calling Michael to tell him, but he didn't pick up, so I just called our agent instead and told her to put in an offer immediately. A few minutes later, Michael called me back (he had been in the shower), asked why I was calling, and I told him I put an offer in on the house across the street. He stuttered at first, completely in shock, and then asked the terms I laid out. They were spot on. "I guess we'll see," he said. We got the house.

Ten years later, that fast-and-loose money decision has made us a half-million dollars.

Another time, we had saved some money to finally do a long-planned remodel project on our home. At this point, our son was about to turn one, and I was four months pregnant with our daughter. I had gone to New York City for my second time ever to attend an exclusive event for ambitious entrepreneurs. After days and days of dreaming big, I was struck with a realization that, while I had all these big dreams, I didn't have any time that was my own to make them come true. I stayed home with our son and would do the same with our daughter, and being a full-time stay-at-home mom leaves very little time to make big business dreams come true.

I remember sneaking out of the ballroom where the event was being held—no one thought twice about it; I'd been peeing incessantly all week—and called Michael. "Hey. You know the money we've been putting aside in the savings account? Why don't we use that money and hire a nanny so I can try to make *more* money?" I wasn't exactly sure *how* I would make money, and admittedly, I was definitely high on all the personal growth Kool-Aid. But something told me it was the right thing to do.

Think about that for a moment. I didn't have a job. My job was to be with the kids. But I wanted to hire someone *else* to be with the kids. So that I could create a job using nothing but my imagination?

After much thought and discussion, we decided to move forward with it, and Sarah started coming to our house several times a week while I went to a local coffee shop or bistro (I would have to pump in the car) to try to create something. It was risky. There was no guarantee it would work. But now, that fast-and-loose money decision has made us millions. The fact that you're reading this right now is the result of a money story that started while standing outside a hotel ballroom and being willing to take a chance.

So, do I play a little fast and loose with money? The stories would tell you yes.

Is that always a bad thing? Tilt them ever so slightly, and the stories will tell you something else.

POT OF GOLDEN STORIES

Like most of us, Amy's money stories have been handed to her. They're a product of her upbringing. She knows she needs to set those stories aside, but what does she replace them with? Amy doesn't have any money stories that she feels will work—she doesn't have any stories of when she was just rolling in dough. It's always been a struggle.

And that's when she finds it.

Amy has plenty of stories of how she emerged on top after a struggle. Could a story whose central plot wasn't necessarily money be a viable story to choose?

The answer is a very big *yes*.

The first story Amy notes is when she first left home and launched her adult life. "Nothing would stop me," she says. "If I wanted to go to Florida for vacation, I'd hop in the car with friends and go to Florida for vacation! I still paid my rent; I just lived a little freer. I didn't sit around and go, 'How am I going to pay my rent this month?' I just did it."

It's a small story but a big deal. I don't think Amy even realizes it, but it directly contradicts what she told me previously—about how she has always had a hard time taking vacations because of the money. This is a story of an Amy who didn't think twice if she wanted to take a vacation—she just *did it*. If Amy wants a little more of that in her life *now,* all she needs to do is tell herself the story of back then.

The next story she brings up is from a little bit later in life, back when her daughters were much younger, and she went through a divorce. She was terrified of what that would mean for her and her two daughters. She didn't want to become a sad, struggling single mom. It was around that time that an entrepreneurial endeavor she had started for fun really began to take off. She was able to keep the home her daughters were raised in. She was able to maintain their quality of life. It was a difficult time, but they thrived through it, all because of her financial abilities.

Another story Amy found was when she decided to change her career and shift into a corporate role. She was well respected by her colleagues, did great work, and made good money doing it.

Finally, Amy found some stories in her current career as an educational consultant for families through an organization she started herself. And while it's not the same as receiving a steady paycheck every other week, the clients keep showing up, and the money keeps coming in.

So many stories. Amy, it turns out, is actually kind of awesome at making money.

In fact, after all the stories, it's a little shocking that she's been struggling with money at all. If I were Amy, I'd be strutting around with the confidence of King Midas. But I shouldn't be surprised. This is why *choosing* can be so challenging—the good stories like to hide. Or at the very least to wrap themselves in the cape of a tough experience, so the good is hard to find. It is also why choosing is such an important part of the process.

Based on what stories Amy has uncovered, stories that *serve* her, a new iceberg statement begins to emerge: "I am always able to make the money I need."

Even when the cards are stacked against her. Even when the mountain seems too steep to climb. Even if it means rising from the ashes or reinventing yourself completely, Amy has never failed to make the money she and her family needs. And *that* is a beautiful thing.

STEP FOUR: INSTALL YOUR CHOSEN STORIES

With this statement as her new North Star, Amy is going to continue to seek out stories that support it. And to make sure she never forgets them again, she's going to officially install them in the front of her mind as a permanent state of being—or at least a more accurate starting point. And, should events occur that trigger old beliefs—hey, it happens—Amy will be prepared.

As you learned in chapter 7, there are some very specific steps for ensuring these new stories stick. I give her the same advice I've given to you—four clear steps:

1. Write down the stories—capture them at least once.
2. Share the stories aloud.
3. Plan for the tough moments.
4. Start each day with your stories.

Amy gets to work. She writes down the stories she had shared with me and includes the components that make a story stick: characters, emotion, a moment, and specific details. She shares her stories aloud with her daughters. She reviews them most mornings and, most challenging of all, she consciously retells herself her chosen stories during the events where she feels most triggered.

As fate would have it, there is no shortage of triggers during the time we're working together. Amy is working on her money story during a particularly triggering time: the holidays and college scholarship/college testing time. Christmas is naturally a time of spending and can be an extremely common trigger for negative money stories. Between Amy's two girls and her husband's three kids, she has five to think about. Add to that the fact that Amy and her husband will have three girls in college at the same time, and just the word *college* is enough to send Amy spiraling back to the "I never have enough money" story.

Amy admits during one of our calls to waking up in the middle of the night, every night, in a panic. Her eyes will shoot open, her heart will race, and within a few moments of being technically awake, her mind will be racing, too. How were they possibly going to have enough money?

But after weeks of actively installing her chosen stories, she notices a change. "Over the last three weeks, I haven't really had any of those moments of fear," she tells me. She also opens an investment account to start to do some stock trading with a little of her spare money. It's something she's always wanted to do—and always *could* have done. Now she's doing it.

Not only that, Amy decides to tell it forward (something we will discuss in chapter 12). Understanding that so many of her challenges with money didn't come from experience but rather were handed down to her, she decides to start changing the stories she tells her daughters. Rather than trying to convince a teenager to retake the ACT to unlock additional scholarship opportunities because "they didn't have enough"—a battle Amy knew she was destined to lose, especially since Amy's mother-in-law had set up a college fund and Amy's daughter naturally thought that was enough—Amy decides to tell her daughter stories about never leaving anything on the table, stories about the pride Amy felt from putting herself through college. Much to Amy's delight, her daughter agreed to retake the test—and in the process, Amy broke the old story of lacking money and created a new story about money and opportunity and abundance.

OH, THE PLACES YOU'LL GO

At the opening of this money discussion, we agreed that money is one of the biggest stories for humankind. Money isn't a thing—it's a story. Here is where I would also like to acknowledge that it is easy for me, a financially stable, white woman in a two-income home, to say that money is a story. To even suggest it may sound flippant or worse, ignorant, if you're currently unemployed, buried in debt, barely able to feed yourself or your family, or if your financial history includes generations of systemic racial oppression, or all of the above. And while I know that all money stories do not begin as equals, the possibility of telling yourself a new story that serves you is available to everyone.

Maybe you've heard of the Law of Attraction—perhaps you've watched *The Secret*. If you *imagine* a million dollars in your bank account, a million dollars will appear. Perhaps you saw that interview with Jim Carrey and Oprah where he admitted to writing a $10 million check to himself, long before he had any material evidence that was possible, dated it Thanksgiving 1995, and put it in his wallet. And the amazement when, just before Thanksgiving 1995, he made $10 million for *Dumb and Dumber*.

Regardless of where you sit on the metaphysical spectrum, it's important to remind you: money is a story, and as such, it can be shaped and shifted simply by your energy around it. And while yes, stories like Jim Carrey's oversimplify it, you now know the *actual* secret.

Your energy can be shifted by simply adjusting the stories you tell yourself.

Money, or lack thereof, is stressful even without a lifetime of potentially negative stories to pull you into a dark hole of panic and hopelessness. I can't tell you the number of times I've felt financial stress, even years into my career. Too many meetings spent sitting down with my key team members to discuss the quarter ahead and why it looks so sparse. Too few events booked. Too few inquiries coming in. Those moments were an immediate cue for my old stories to enter stage right: "You are bad at money. You always spend too much and then don't have enough." The stories would crowd the room and cloud my judgment. My immediate instinct was to do *more*—more outreach, more emails, more saying yes, thereby compromising myself and my worth in the process. Every call that came in became life and death, feast or famine.

I can only imagine what potential clients were thinking on the other side of our sales calls—I'm sure they heard my words, but the energy with which I was *saying* them probably spoke more loudly and, let's be honest, frantic desperation disguised as a sales pitch is *not* a good look.

Then, without even realizing I was doing it, I started working on my self-stories about money. It turns out, the times I took my biggest financial "risks" were the times that created the most financial abundance. Story after story, just a couple of which I've already shared with you here, each of them ending with, "The money will come. Keep doing you, and the money will come."

I remember one team meeting, in particular. We were in New York City in a coworking space when my business manager revealed the not-so-great numbers of the coming month. After she shared the news, an uncomfortable silence hung in the room as everyone paused and waited for me to speak. I took a breath, quickly told myself a few of my chosen stories, and responded, "The right clients will come. We are doing the right things. We will keep doing the right things for the right reasons, and the clients (and money) will come."

Our meeting adjourned shortly after, and each of us checked our emails as we exited the conference room. "Whoa," my business manager said. "You won't believe this . . . but three inquiries came in while we were in that meeting! And they look good!"

Even when facing my darkest financial days in the spring of 2020 when hundreds of thousands of dollars vanished overnight—it turns out being a keynote speaker for live events in front of twenty thousand people is not a great business to be in in the age of isolation and social distancing—I still had a sense of knowing that this was the middle of a story I would tell someday. While there were more than enough reasons to panic, and I certainly did partake in a few moments of complete financial terror, I still felt a sense of peace. I was laying my golden road of positive financial stories as fast as I could, placing them in a repeating pattern to create a path that, yes, took a short detour but quickly corrected course to the Emerald City I knew I was destined to reach.

I get that the spiritual conversations about money can be a little too much. However, you can still tap into the power they offer without having to go too far down the new-age rabbit hole. Simply understanding and retelling yourself *true* stories about money, stories that *serve* you, can be all the cosmic shift you need—or at least it can be a start.

It was for Amy.

As we wrapped up our final session together, I could tell a lot had changed for Amy. She was more in control, more relaxed, and, most tangible of all, Amy had the best first week of January in her business to date. "I have clients coming out of everywhere," she said. "Whatever this is, I'm going to continue doing it. I've got my energy in the right place."

Out of curiosity, I looked back at my notes from our very first session, where she identified one of her iceberg statements as, "Where is the next client coming from?"

The answer, it would seem, is from a new story.

11

RELATIONSHIPS AND LOVE

Connecting with the Characters of Life

I've lived my whole life believing the bad stories,
and for the first time, I paid attention to the good ones.

—JULIA

I almost cut this chapter.

Almost didn't include it at all.

In my group of participants, only two of them joined with
the intention of working on relationship stories. One of them
was struggling to find love after heartbreak, and at the end of
our second session, I questioned whether the self-storytelling
method was helping or hurting her more. My concerns were
all but confirmed when she wrote me a week later and said she
needed to talk.

I couldn't sleep that night, and by the morning, I had decided
that maybe self-storytelling and relationships was just too much
to tackle.

I wasn't wrong. The role of storytelling in relationships is a
huge thing. Life *is* relationships between humans, and if humans
are made of stories in much the same way we are made of cells (a
safe conclusion to draw now, eleven chapters in), then relationships
are *those* stories exponentially multiplied by the people involved.

How, I wondered, could the scope of human relationships be
covered in a single chapter? It deserves a book of its own. The

storyteller in my head suggested *maybe you should just hold off for a bit.*

Then I had that fateful conversation with the participant who messaged me.

And when it took an unexpected turn, a story I will share with you in just a few paragraphs from now, I knew this was one of the most important chapters of all.

Because while every one of your relationships, be it familial, professional, friendship, romantic, or otherwise, involves at least two people, one of them is always *you.* Armed with what you now know, you have the power to positively impact the connections you have with others, which will, in turn, positively impact the world.

There is no reason to wait for that.

So let's not.

EVERYONE HAS A STORY

I can't watch the first few minutes of the movie *Up* without bawling.

I've tried. I fail every time.

And then, once I finally sniffle my way past the initial sadness of a man I barely know losing the love of his life, there comes a scene where the bad guys are trying to take the old man's house, and they mess with the mailbox the old man and the love-of-his-life painted decades earlier, and the old man gets so upset and whaps the bad guy on the head with his cane. And then the old guy has to go to court, and the judge does not rule in his favor and every. single. time. I want to yell at the television (and sometimes I do): *"If you knew his story, you would understand!"*

Of course, this isn't only true for the Pixar masterpiece; it's true in real life, too, and we know it. Our unknown, untold stories impact our interpersonal connections—both long-term relationships and fleeting ones—on a daily basis.

Stories on a Plane

I've mentioned more than once the big role travel has played in my life. In 2019, I took so many flights that I achieved Executive Platinum on American Airlines, Diamond on Delta, and even (reluctantly) gained a little status on United. Basically, I was in the air more than I was on the ground, and I'd be lying if I said it didn't wear on me.

One afternoon I boarded a little plane and mistakenly thought a woman was sitting in my seat. I politely said, "Excuse me, I think you are in my seat." But I was wrong. And she was *furious* that I had made that mistake. She was *so* furious, in fact, that she called her friend once I sat down and told her friend how a woman had lost her mind and said she was in the wrong seat and who does she think she is? (Since I was sitting *right next to her,* she could have asked.)

If she'd only understood that it was my tenth flight in half as many days and I was delirious with stress and missing my family and simply misread the sign above the seat and reversed the window and aisle. If she had known my story, or if I had had the energy to tell it once she hung up the phone, maybe she would have acted with more compassion. And, of course, if I had had the energy to ask for *her* story, maybe I would have understood why she reacted so strongly and that her reaction wasn't actually *about* me, but rather a much bigger story buried within her.

But neither one of us did that.

Strangers are a part of our lives, and yet sometimes, one negative interaction from a person I don't know and will never see again has the power to completely throw me off my game. And it's just as true of digital encounters. Ever had a negative comment from an internet troll set you off for a day, or worse, incite an unwarranted interrogation that leaves you questioning yourself?

This response, this surrendering of your precious energy to a complete and irrelevant stranger, makes no sense. But that doesn't seem to keep it from happening. And until we can make ourselves immune to these surprise attacks, the next best thing I have found is the acknowledgment of self-storytelling on two different levels.

The first is to recognize that their behavior isn't the problem—the problem is that the behavior has triggered one of the stories you carry with you. A troll on YouTube leaving a nasty comment about the song you posted, for example, could trigger your inner stories that tell you you aren't good enough. The woman on the plane that day tapped into my deep inner storyteller, who berates me for not being perfect.

The second acknowledgment is that they, too, have a story. Your posting of the song triggers the troll's stories that keep him from posting his *own* song that he's been working on. The woman on the plane might have grown up with a whole chorus of people telling her she was wrong when, in fact, she wasn't.

Recognizing that self-stories are always being told is the first step in stopping random moments from turning into unnecessary downward spirals and, more importantly, the first step toward a world of more empathy and patience.

SEEK OUT STORIES

Have you ever had to deal with a difficult person at work? I can practically *hear* the short output of breath as you think to yourself: *Um. Duh.*

Difficult people are an inevitable part of life because people are inevitably difficult. And while it would be great if we could cull our offices, job sites, or Slack channels of the people we can't seem to stand, it's simply not possible.

Instead, lean into what you now know about self-storytelling. Remember, each person has within them a lifetime of stories that are influencing how they respond to the world around them—a world that includes the people on their team. Your job is to seek out as many of those stories as you can in an effort to understand these behaviors better.

Brené Brown said, "People are hard to hate close up. Move in." Abraham Lincoln wisely stated, "I don't like that man. I must get to know him better." And you've likely seen, perhaps even shared, the meme that implores you to be kind to others because you never know the extent of someone else's story. While understanding your stories helps you to respond to events in more positive, productive ways, understanding the inner stories of others helps do the same—and that can go a long way at work.

I worked with a woman years ago who, for some reason, I struggled to build consistent rapport with. One minute we seemed totally in a groove—working together for hours immersed in moving a big initiative forward. And then, a few days later, she wouldn't speak to me. I would see her in the office, and it was like I wasn't even there. Then, I would spend days retracing my steps, trying to figure out what went wrong.

I wasn't the only one who struggled in my relationship with her. Many of our colleagues had already given up and only worked with her when they had to, but they never allowed themselves to get too close and suggested I do the same.

I almost took their advice; the relational whiplash was draining my energy and affecting my work. But then one day, completely by accident, the woman told me a story. It was the story of a particular event in her life, a story about trust and betrayal, and one that drastically shaped her as a person. And after she told me that story, everything changed. I understood her more, and when she behaved the way she did, I was able to see that behavior not as a response to me, but rather a response driven by story. Because of that understanding, I was able to allow more space for grace and compassion, which in turn created a positive spiral that led to more trust between the two of us, and ultimately a better working relationship.

That's what stories do. They allow room for grace, patience, and progress. Bringing the inner stories out helps to dissolve misunderstandings, big or small, and even keep them from occurring in the first place. If ever you find yourself in a difficult working relationship, and quitting your job isn't really an option, try seeking out the self-stories. Not only will they help you to understand your colleague better, but they will also allow you to separate yourself from their response—especially if you have a tendency to internalize others' behaviors.

It's that separation of selves and stories that makes all the difference.

UNTANGLING YOUR STORY FROM THEIRS

In one of our group check-ins during the self-storytelling research project, the participants started sharing that, not only were they seeing changes within themselves, but also a change in the way they understand others' behaviors. From why a father was distant to why a sister wasn't supportive, to why a wife was closed off. Realizing that someone's behavior is much more about *their* stories than *you* can be a huge relief and total liberation.

I'll never forget the conversations I had with my parents, especially my father, regarding our move to New York City. You remember Mike, don't you?

I was in my midthirties, a married mother of two with a great career and a solid head on my shoulders. For whatever reason, city living was calling to us and even though, I'll admit, from the outside it might seem a little crazy, it worked for us . . . but not for my father.

I remember the baffled tone in his voice as he sat in the "dream home" we had just purchased a few years earlier. The home that backed up to the private golf course to which we belonged. The kids' school was the best in the state and just around the corner from us. We were fifteen minutes from the airport. We had a whole community and a lot of family there . . . why would we ever want to leave?! He just couldn't wrap his head around it and wasn't afraid to let me know it.

And I'll admit, it wasn't easy for me, even as a grown woman, to proceed with something that my father was so adamantly opposed to and led to some second-guessing and self-doubt. But then I remembered *his* inner storyteller, the one who prefers safety. The one that says security is the goal. The one that kept him at his job instead of pursuing other, riskier options. Our move was driving my father's inner storyteller insane! I had to untangle my father's stories from my own. And while having his full support from the start would have been nice, it simply wasn't something his self-stories would allow.

It's important to note, there is no right and wrong here. There are simply two different sets of self-stories. Recognizing and honoring that is the most effective way of moving forward.

Even those participants who didn't enter the research project with the intention of working on their relationship stories had similar realizations about the power of untangling the self-stories of others from their own. Often, the challenge they wanted to address in their lives involved someone else—someone with their own stories and therefore perspectives and beliefs about how life should be lived. The feeling of freedom when you are able to untangle your story from someone else's and find ways for both of them to exist as they are is worth every ounce of effort.

IT'S SO HARD TO SAY GOODBYE

Finally, and most difficult of all, sometimes you have no choice but to let go of a bad character.

Not so many years ago, I was *so* excited to tell one of my dear friends the good news: Michael and I were pregnant! I'm sure we chatted about other things for a moment or two first before I simply couldn't contain myself. "I'm pregnant!" I said. Then I waited for her reaction, my face frozen in a gigantic smile, eyebrows raised all the way to my hairline.

A look flashed across her face. Was it disgust? Disdain? Disappointment? Whatever it was, it certainly wasn't happiness. In my confusion, I asked, "What?" Was there something stuck in my teeth? Had someone ordered brussels sprouts, and the smell had offended her? *Something* else must be going on because *what friend makes that face when someone shares they're going to have a baby?*

"Oh." She shrugged. "I've just seen so many of my ambitious friends get pregnant and then stop whatever they're doing to just be moms."

I'd love to say that she said it with a "but I believe in you!" tone. Or that she followed up her statement with, "You can make all your dreams come true!" but she did not. It was definitely a "You just ruined your life" tone to which I wanted to ask: So what do you suggest I do? Send the baby back?!

I don't remember the rest of the conversation. But I *do* remember it was the beginning of my realization that she often said things like that—seemingly supportive but subtly hurtful things. Like the time I had been really working on getting in shape and making good food choices, and when we ordered Thai food but I only ate half of mine, she hissed something about me being anorexic. Or the day a great opportunity came up for me at work, and she said in a snide tone, "Don't forget us little people."

Eventually, I decided I just didn't want that in my life anymore. It was hard—it's hard to step away from someone who has become a part of your story, a person you care for and hang out with. But I had no choice. It was her or me, and I chose me.

Over time, I just stopped saying yes to lunches, and dinners, and coffees. I wasn't angry or vengeful. I was just done with that chapter of my story. And though it wasn't easy to say no to her, it felt really good to say yes to *me*.

If there is a character in your life who frowns at your most exciting news or whose "support" feels like it might be criticism in disguise, you have my permission to end their chapter in your story. I am also sending you a few extra hugs because you're probably going to need them. (And now if only I could find some of the ambition I lost since having children.)

REWRITING YOUR LOVE STORY

Meet Julia.

I've been patiently waiting for you to meet Julia, and I am so excited the time has finally come.

I met Julia at LaGuardia Airport in the late summer of 2019. The terminal had just been redone—it was beautiful, and I was sitting at the bar of one of the new bistros that would make you forget the frustration of a delayed flight or the subtle sadness that comes from living out of your suitcase. A young woman wearing a baseball cap a few stools down called out, "Excuse me. How do you get your hair to look like that?"

We chatted the way that two travelers crossing paths and enjoying mimosas tend to do. We compared flights. Complained about the infuriating airport construction and then marveled at the terminal masterpiece and contemplated whether it was all worth it. We discussed how to style her new shorter hair. And, after noticing my wedding ring, she confessed she wanted one of her own. We talked about heartbreak and what good love feels like.

And then, just like that, our time was over. Julia's plane began boarding, and then mine. We caught our flights, and our chance connection had come to an end.

But Julia left an impression on me. I loved her openness and how willing she was to proclaim, to a stranger, her desire for love. I've known many "Julias" in my life—male Julias, female Julias, young Julias, and Julias with six-plus decades under their belts. In fact, I *am* a Julia. I started my search for big, bold, exquisite love in kindergarten and can name every boy who was in the running until the day Michael Hall kissed me the first time. Ask any person, no matter their age, gender, or orientation; the search for true love is arduous and one to be taken seriously.

Julia and I might never have crossed paths again if it weren't for social media. More than a year later, when I was launching the research project for this book, Julia applied to join the program, just as I hoped she would.

During our first one-on-one session, Julia caught me up on what had happened in her love life since the first (and last) time we'd spoken—a catch-up that focused on one man.

Ryan.

Not long after our chance meeting, Julia was sitting on a flight and, in that special way Julia can, struck up a conversation with the woman sitting next to her. By the end of the flight, and being totally enamored by Julia's quest for big beautiful love, the woman had a moment of inspiration. "I know the most wonderful man. You would *love* him," the woman exclaimed. "And he will love you." Usually these chance encounters fizzle once the travelers step away from the baggage carousel, but three days later, Julia walked into an oyster bar and there he was.

And even though she didn't like oysters, she immediately knew there was something different about him. The conversation was so easy, like they'd known each other forever, and though Julia never kisses on a first date, he kissed her goodnight. The next day, Julia was back at the airport on another trip and they talked every night they were apart—three hours, five hours, they couldn't get enough of each other. By the time she arrived back in Texas, Julia knew . . . This was it.

That was October of 2019, and over the next several months, the two fell even more in love. Ryan was equal parts logical and loving. While he opened every door and always reached for her hand, he was also the hardest working, most driven and determined man she'd ever known. "He graduated with a finance degree from a prestigious Texas institution and then worked his way up from the oil field to a coveted white-collar position—something he had always dreamed of," Julia told me. The pride oozed from her, even through the screen.

It was all so perfect, and then it all changed. The oil industry was hit hard by the pandemic. Ryan lost his job, then his truck and apartment, which were both parts of the package. Everything he worked so hard for vanished overnight. As someone who had high expectations for his life and a strong desire to provide with and for a partner, the collapse of his career necessitated the end of their relationship. "In his eyes, he was not the man I needed him to be. Using that beautiful, logical brain I loved so much, Ryan determined that he was not in a position to be in a relationship of this magnitude. He had to let me go."

Before she could wrap her head around what was happening, they went from being in love to being over.

"I went from the happiest I've ever been in my life," Julia recalled, "to the most heartbroken."

That was seven months before joining the research project. When she came to me, Julia was ready to begin again, to find the love she knew was possible. And yet, there seemed to be an invisible barrier. Something that, for her whole life, save for a few glimpses of hope and moments of love (Ryan being one of them), had kept her from getting there.

You, of course, know what this barrier is: self-stories.

STEP ONE: CATCH YOUR STORIES AT WORK

The very first thing Julia was tasked to do was to catch her stories—to look for those statements that were so ingrained, so automatic, and so definitive, but so overlooked and unattended. For our first session, she came with a list of phrases she frequently said to herself, and it wasn't pretty:

- "I am unworthy."
- "I am undeserving of love."

- "I am an inconvenience."
- "I am not worth fighting for."

These statements in and of themselves were obvious obstacles on a path to a healthy, loving relationship. So obvious, in fact, that one might be tempted to fight fire with fire, or in this case, statement with statement. She could have written, "I am worthy of love, I am deserving of love," a hundred times a day in a journal in the morning like a fifth-grader writing sentences on a chalkboard as both punishment and an attempt to change.

Let me ask you: Did writing "I will not talk in class" one hundred times ever keep you quiet?

I didn't think so. And it doesn't work here either.

Perhaps, then, if Julia wanted to bring out the big guns, she could create a vision board with photos and images cut out from magazines. Gorgeous men embracing gorgeous women on the beach with the sunset in the background as a source of inspiration for the kind of relationship she was seeking.

But, as you've come to know, and as Julia learned in the process, her statements were just the tips of much larger, more ominous story icebergs. A few sentences or photographs alone weren't going to be enough to steer her ship off into the sunset to live happily ever after with the love of her life.

Willing to fully engage in the method, Julia took a deep breath and set out to find the stories keeping her beliefs afloat. Being a self-aware adult, she had a pretty good sense of where to start.

STEP TWO: ANALYZE YOUR SELF-STORIES

Julia was raised by her father's family. Her father was eighteen when she was born, and her birth mother left shortly after (Julia wouldn't meet her birth mother until she was twenty years old).

However, despite the nontraditional circumstances, Julia looks back on that time with love. She was raised by her father, grandmother, and aunt, attended private school in Queens, and took as many dance classes as her little feet could handle.

But even with all that love, there was a plot twist in her story. Her young father eventually fell in love again, married, had three more children, and moved to Brooklyn and eventually upstate New York while Julia stayed in Queens with her grandmother and aunts. And though she loves her family and is so grateful for them, she could acknowledge that, just miles away, there was a picture-perfect family unit that was technically hers but that she couldn't fully be a part of all the time. Even though her father and his wife (the only woman Julia ever called Mom) loved her and wanted her, and her grandmother loved and wanted her, the circumstances became a natural environment for stories that could make one feel like an inconvenience.

Then there were the stories of a previous long-term relationship. Julia spent years attending her boyfriend's family birthday parties and work events, and would go above and beyond to socialize and make a good impression. But when it was an event for Julia, her boyfriend wouldn't show. He refused to attend anything that mattered to Julia.

There was the Sunday of Julia's friend's birthday party. They were going on a Malibu Wine Safari and had been planning it for weeks. Her boyfriend loved wine, and Julia was sure he would want to go, but when the day arrived, her boyfriend decided he simply wasn't in the mood. Julia begged, pleaded, cried—she wanted so desperately for her friends to meet her boyfriend—but in the end, Julia went alone.

I am undeserving of love. I am not worth the effort.

The stories were all there, and Julia could retell them in vivid detail.

STEP THREE: CHOOSE A STORY THAT SERVES YOU

Having caught sight of the stories that didn't serve her, it was time to find ones that would. I asked Julia to look for stories in her past of when she *had* felt deserving in relationships and deserving of love.

For many people, this is easier said than done. A common pitfall when we begin to look for the powerful and positive stories in our life is to discount what we find. We add caveats. We downplay the events. We attribute the stories to something outside ourselves, like that one lucky break or the influence of someone else.

Julia faced that challenge, even stating, "There are so many good stories—why have I been telling myself only the bad ones for so long?"

But for Julia, there was another challenge, one that might sound familiar to anyone who has found great love only to have it vanish overnight. All of Julia's *good* stories—the stories of feeling loved, of feeling worthy of love—also involved Ryan, the man responsible for her heartbreak.

We were at a storytelling crossroads.

If you were to listen to the recording of our second interview, you would hear me struggling. Lots of *ums*, lots of long pauses. Lots of trying to find the right words and knowing that, even if the words are right, the direction might be wrong. Here was a woman who was still clearly in love with a man who, seven months earlier, had made it clear that their relationship was over. And here I was, about to encourage her to keep telling herself the stories of the good times they had.

"There are a couple of different ways we could go." I paused. In the video, I looked around, I chewed my pen, I fidgeted as I debated what to say next. Finally, I said: "There are a couple of ways we could go. One of those ways is to tell yourself that, since that relationship is over, it means that you didn't mean anything to that person. That there wasn't love there. That there is something wrong with us. That we are flawed, unworthy, not worth fighting for."

Julia nodded. In fact, she'd already been telling herself those stories. "I made up stories about how he was doing," she said. "How he didn't give a shit about me anymore."

"But . . ." I took a breath, decisive. "That version of those stories isn't going to serve you going *forward*. I understand that telling yourself the good stories of a relationship that is over can hurt . . . but, it's better than deleting them or twisting them into *bad* stories . . . because that version of the story becomes about what is wrong with *you*. And we don't need that. We don't need you thinking that there's something wrong with you. That is already your default. What we *need* are the stories of the times where you *did* experience love. Where you felt worthy and lovable.

"I understand if that is just too hard," I cautioned. "But I want you to give it a try. Because the day will come, when you're sitting at the airport and the perfect guy comes up to you and strikes up a conversation, and at that moment, I want the stories playing in your mind to be stories that say, 'Yes! I am worthy of big, beautiful love and maybe this is it!' instead of, 'Well, this will obviously end badly.'"

We ended the session, and when my camera turned off, I sighed and shook my head.

Maybe I was all wrong.

Maybe I just told a hurting woman to replay the best memories with the man who had broken her heart.

From a story-theory perspective, I felt it was the right move. But from a practical perspective, I might have just sent her deep into a cave full of Ben & Jerry's to yell at rom-coms. And, as I revealed at the start of the chapter, my worst fears were seemingly confirmed when I received a message from Julia saying we needed to have a conversation. It had been a few days since I'd heard from her, and I assumed this was her way of exiting the self-storytelling experience. It was in that period of silence I decided I should probably drop this chapter all together.

I couldn't have been more wrong.

LOVING YOURSELF FIRST

You've no doubt heard it before: "Before you can be loved by someone else, you must first love yourself." Or the similar version, "You can only give love to others if you love yourself first." The phrase makes sense, and I don't know many people who would disagree that self-love is an important first step to love in general. The question, of course, is, *how*? How do you love yourself? How do you believe you are worthy of love? How do you rewire your brain to increase the flow of self-love and decrease the constant supply of self-loathing?

Julia will tell you it is through stories. "We've all heard the importance of changing our negative thoughts into positive ones . . . but focusing on *stories*, instead of just *thoughts*, makes it more tangible. You're not just saying, 'Oh, think positive," but instead, you're replaying things that actually happened. Things that were *real*. There's power in that." These were the thoughts she shared on our group call before our third one-on-one call, which she eventually scheduled.

I forgave her for the tardiness. She had been busy, it seemed.

Busy falling back in love with Ryan.

I was as shocked as anyone when I realized that Julia's lack of response was *not* because choosing stories was too hard, but because she chose them, and they *worked*. She decided that, even though Ryan was the main character in all her good stories and it was heartbreaking that they weren't together, Ryan really was the first time she had felt loved, seen, worthy, and appreciated.

"Even if I never saw him again, which was what I was expecting," Julia shared, "he's the first person that made me really feel all those things that I haven't felt about myself. So, even if it were to be with someone else, I know it's possible now. That's what the stories helped me to realize . . . and it *changed* me."

She wrote down the story of when he had coronavirus and was so grateful for her taking care of him. She wrote down the story of the first time they met. Of the first time he told her he loved her. She worked to choose the good stories over the bad ones, and in doing so, changed the fundamental beliefs she had about herself.

STEP FOUR: INSTALL YOUR CHOSEN STORIES

Julia was diligent about installing her new stories once she found them, including inserting them where the old, negative stories would have otherwise been triggered. The sight of happy couples became a sign of hope and possibility. Even her barstools became transformed "triggers."

"I love my blue velvet barstools, I really do. But we broke up sitting in those barstools, and every time I looked at them, I thought about that." Julia started inserting some of her chosen stories instead. "Instead of looking at them and telling myself the story of our breakup, I looked at them and told myself the stories of all the meals we shared sitting on these barstools. I told myself about the times he said 'I love you' sitting in these barstools." Julia smiled. "There were some great stories here, and even though it was dangerous, telling myself the *good* stories rewired my brain, and over time . . . I just felt stronger. I felt better. I *believed* that love was real, that I deserved it, and that I would find it again."

As the year came to an end, Julia decided to reach out to Ryan—regardless of what might come. "It's Christmas," she said. "And this was my last effort. The stories made me confident enough."

To her surprise, the talk went well, and they agreed to meet a few days later for coffee. That, too, went well, and Julia realized that the stories she'd been telling herself about how Ryan felt about her post-breakup—that he didn't care, that he had forgotten her— were fiction. He was just as heartbroken and lonely as she was.

In short order, the relationship that Julia thought was lost forever had been restored. Almost immediately, sitting together on the blue velvet barstools, Ryan invited her home for Christmas to meet his family.

HAPPILY EVER AFTER, NO MATTER WHAT

At the time this chapter was written, Julia and Ryan are still very much in love. Yes, they've had their challenges—new jobs, new schedules, adjusting to the still uncertain times following 2020. But Julia sounds like a different person than the woman I met at the LaGuardia Airport. "I just don't let myself go there anymore," she says confidently. A missed call, a moment of frustration doesn't equate to a deluge of "he loves me not" stories. "I can spiral hard. I'm an emotional person—it's one of the best things about me and, for a long time, was one of my biggest challenges. But now, with these stories, I feel like I have my power back." And while Julia believes it will stay that way, even if things change, her new story won't.

In our final session, I read Julia's original statements back to her: "I am unworthy. I am undeserving of love. I am an inconvenience. I am not worth fighting for." And I asked her how it felt now, hearing those phrases. She paused.

"It makes me feel really sad . . ." She took a breath. "Obviously. That's sad . . . But you know, I feel powerful that I was able to take that sorrow and take those broken pieces and make something from that." I asked her if they still seemed as true as they had six weeks earlier when she first said them.

"They feel big because they were a huge part of my life for a really long time . . ." Another pause. And then, Julia finished. "But for the first time, when you just said them, they felt like the past. They still feel big. But they feel like they are for someone else. For the first time, I feel like I am leaving that woman behind."

12

FAMILY AND PARENTING

Telling It Forward

We can't really give to our children what we don't have
ourselves. In that sense, my greatest gift to my daughter is
that I continue to work on myself.

—MARIANNE WILLIAMSON

That's a quote from *A Return to Love*—a book released in 1992
that achieved mass recognition when praised by Oprah Winfrey.
As a first-time reader nearly thirty years later, I was hanging on
every word and that passage, in particular, jumped off the page
and pierced my exhausted heart. I admit to translating it slightly
through a storytelling lens to read:

*"In that sense, my greatest gift to my children is that I continue to work
on the stories I tell myself."*

And while *all* stories matter when it comes to becoming an
overall better version of yourself, I've found that the stories I tell
myself about my role, and ultimately my ability, as a parent need
extra attention.

The role of parent, guardian, or primary role model in a child's
life is impossibly big, and no job is more storied. Knowing how
many of the stories we tell ourselves are handed down by our
mother and father figures, the pressure is on from the moment
that a child arrives in your care. Self-stories will undoubtedly help
you rise to the challenge.

But this is where the method also extends beyond *you*.

When it comes to family and parenting, every story you tell becomes a tool not just for you but for the children in your care—equipping them with better stories to tell *themselves*, and eventually, to tell others. There's no better place to begin a world-changing story movement.

PUTTING YOUR OXYGEN MASK ON FIRST

There is no tougher job than raising another human, and yet, there is no instruction manual. I remember packing up the hospital room when the realization hit me that we were taking the baby with us; he was ours to care for. I felt like whispering to a nurse, "You know that I don't know how to do this, right? Are you sure it's safe for us to go?" Instead, I sat in the back seat and yelled, *"slow down"* at Michael the whole way home despite the fact that he never broke thirty miles an hour.

Imposter syndrome comes up a lot in conversations about work and career. I don't hear it as often in parenting because I think, on some level, we know and accept our inexperience. But the lurking iceberg of having no idea what you're doing never fully goes away, even after decades of trying. It's a breeding ground for negative stories to grow and take over. Add to it social apps, the media, the perfect parents who are never late to drop-off or pickup, and the stories of your *own* childhood, and how can anyone ever feel like they've reached the Emerald City of parenting?

Fortunately, the same four steps of the self-storytelling method apply to this complicated job.

STEP ONE: CATCH YOUR STORIES AT WORK

As I've shared, this was one of the areas where I struggled. I watched the mothers around me who made lunches that looked like art and hosted birthday parties that belonged on television. I replayed every forgotten snack day, every gymnastics showcase I watched via FaceTime, every classroom Valentine's Day party, and every missed field trip in vivid detail. I constantly told myself I was a bad mom, that I was selfish, that I was somehow doing it wrong because I wasn't doing it like everyone else.

STEP TWO: ANALYZE YOUR SELF-STORIES

If you were to look at the Christmas photos from my childhood, you would assume holiday spirit was in my genes. You'd see images of handmade Christmas outfits, of Christmas cookies baked from ancestral recipes, of the ornaments my siblings and I made each year (yes, I still have my clothespin Dorothy ornament).

There would be videos of us singing carols—"O Holy Night," "Silent Night," "Joy to the World," and, every once in a while, the sacrilegious "Rudolph the Red-Nosed Reindeer." The traditions started the Saturday after Thanksgiving and continued, like clock-work, until December 26—even *that* day became a tradition as The Day We Did Whatever We Wanted.

So, if the moms at school drop-off weren't enough, I had another story to tell myself—one about my perfect mother. And while I know she wasn't *actually* perfect, there are plenty of vivid stories my memory draws on when it searches for evidence of my parental shortcomings, particularly when it came to holiday traditions.

As I reached adulthood and had a family of my own, these sto-ries mutated from sweet memories into standards I feared I could never achieve. I didn't know how to bake the cookies of my ances-tors. I was terrible with arts and crafts. And my son, who attended a nonreligious charter school for kindergarten, insisted that "My Country 'Tis of Thee" was a Christmas carol.

I had a pretty good sense that the holiday spirit did *not* flow through my veins. Maybe it skipped a generation. But it didn't matter if I wasn't naturally blessed; the incredible stories of my youth made me feel as if great holiday traditions were what made a great parent.

And so I was determined to start one of my own.

STEP THREE: CHOOSE A STORY THAT SERVES YOU

One holiday season, now well aware of the stories I knew were keeping me from fully enjoying motherhood *my* way, I decided to choose a different story. However, lacking content sufficient to *replace* what was there, I decided to create a whole new story from scratch.

I had heard about an *experience*—it was called The North Pole Experience. Essentially, you pay a bunch of money and head to a place in the mountains where you catch a trolley that takes you to a portal that transports you to Santa's workshop.

"This sounds like a tradition if I've ever heard one!" I thought as I took out my credit card and ignored the price tag. No expense would be spared in an effort to secure this story.

When the day finally arrived, we bundled the kids up, piled into our car, and began the drive up into the mountains to meet the trolley. The tickets explicitly warned us not to be late—the trolley left promptly, and any stragglers would forfeit their voyage. I didn't think much of it; I'd been up to the general spot in these mountains before, and we left with an hour and a half until boarding. It wasn't until we were in the car that I decided to enter in the exact address on our GPS. As I did, Siri announced in a tone that I'm quite certain was meant to mock me:

"You will arrive at your destination in two hours."

Two hours? Two hours! We were already on our way, and we still had two hours to go? I started to panic as my mother's holiday tradition stories flashed before my eyes.

We weren't going to make the trolley. My kids weren't going to go to the North Pole. How could I have messed this up? I looked over at Michael, who was driving, and who picked up the pace ever so slightly. I looked into the back seat at my kids—they were happily chatting about what they thought the North Pole would look like and what they thought they might do.

And that's when I realized—

They had no idea.

They had no idea what the North Pole Experience was *supposed* to be, so they would have no idea if it looked a little different than the website where I spent a small fortune on the tickets. The tickets for the experience that we were now going to miss because I was a terrible mother.

So I prepared a story.

It turns out that the North Pole, when you first get there, looks a lot like Home Depot. And when you walk in, you can pick your own Santa hat—they just have racks of them! You choose one, put it on your head, and then, magically, there are rows of pre-lit Christmas trees that you can walk through. It's the . . . the . . . it's the North Pole Forest! And in the forest, there are lines of lit-up snowmen and reindeer that move their heads. Isn't this amazing, children?!

And then! You can walk through the elves' workshop, where all the lumber is. Oh wow! Look at all the lumber. Stacks and stacks of lumber! Yes, the elves went home to be with their families, that's why you don't see them right now. They're not here but look at all the wood for all the toys.

And the Christmas light fixture aisle—I mean . . . festive workshop area. Look how the lights bring light and joy to all the world!

It gets better! Once you pay for the Santa hats and you leave, you can head down the street to where Santa's coffee shop is. What's that? Yes, Santa also loves Starbucks. And you can get two children's hot chocolates with marshmallows in them and even a special snowman cookie or North Pole cake pop.

And did you know that at the North Pole, the neighbors love Christmas carolers? Yes! We can walk up and down the streets of the North Pole neighborhood, singing "Rudolph the Red-Nosed Reindeer" and "My Country 'Tis of Thee." And then we can pull the blanket out of the back of our car that we were supposed to take on a picnic one summer (but I'm not good at picnics either), and we would find a famous North Pole park and lie down and look up at the stars and make special North Pole wishes that *always* come true.

There are times when being a storyteller is a big advantage.

Yes, I was ready. As Michael drove faster, I googled Home Depots in the nearest towns should we pull up to the trolley just as it was pulling away.

As it turns out, it was a story I didn't have to tell. A combination of very little traffic, skilled driving, and a trolley that wasn't as punctual as it threatened to be meant we made it in time.

STEP FOUR: INSTALL YOUR CHOSEN STORIES

In the end, the real North Pole Experience was fine. But as we drove home that night, looking at the stars through the windshield and two sleeping babies in the back, I wondered if maybe it wasn't about the experience that you buy or the cookies that you bake or the traditions that you try to have. Maybe it's actually about the stories. The ones that you make along the way.

That year, I pulled out the box of ornaments that my siblings and I had made over the course of decades under my mother's loving eye. My son and daughter pulled each one out of the box and asked for the story. And I told it to them. And in the process, we created a new story together.

Whether you grew up with stories you wish to never re-create or stories you feel you never can, you have stories that will serve. You have stories of times where you've been caring. Or patient. Generous. Loving. Determined. The times you've had clear boundaries. When you've done the right thing even when it felt hard.

Those are the stories that make great parents because great parents are simply people with stories about doing their best.

THE NEW BEDTIME STORY

After all this talk about the stories that you, an adult, tell yourself, I want to take a moment to remind you how much *children* love stories. Kids love stories even more than we grown-ups do. Stories are the number one culprit when it comes to bedtime routines that overstay their welcome and movies that are requested way too many times.

In *Stories That Stick*, I shared the story of my son's obsession with the book *Goodnight, Goodnight, Construction Site*, and that the only escape from me drowning in a gravel pit from too many readings was to tell him one of my *own* stories about catching fireflies as a kid.

Children are sponges for stories. Yet, for all their power, we rarely use stories to the extent we could with our children. We'll read a bedtime story to put them to sleep, but when we try to teach important life lessons, we resort to simple statements or rules instead of the magical stories that kids love so much.

Can you take what you now know about stories and *proactively* equip children with better ones? The answer is most certainly *yes*.

The Pasta Night Problem

When my son was five, he was invited by a friend to a pasta night at a local club. Technically, it would be his first excursion without his family, and while I took it as just another playdate but with more food, I was surprised to find that he was nervous.

After some discussion, I discovered that he was really just anxious about the "newness" of it all. He'd be going to a new place, doing a new thing. And more than anything, he was nervous about the pasta itself. What kind would it be? What if it was a new kind of pasta he didn't like?

Yes. The shape of the noodles was his primary concern.

In the hours leading up to his departure, I assured him everything would be fine, then again as I loaded him into the other family's vehicle, then he waved to me out the open window while driving away.

As you might guess, everything *was* fine. In fact, it was *better* than fine. It turns out pasta night included bouncy houses and games and, yes, all different kinds of pasta, including his favorite.

That night at bedtime, I had him tell me the whole story from beginning to end. Everything from, to borrow the framework I discuss in *Stories that Stick*, the "normal" or beginning of the story (his nerves about pasta night) to the "explosion" of actually going to pasta night. And finally, the "new normal"—how he learned that new things can be fun. We gave the experience an unofficial name, *The Big Pasta Adventure*—a fun story with a happy ending, followed by a great night's sleep.

A few weeks later, it was time for another rite of passage for my young son: kindergarten screening. This was a process at the local school where they interview each incoming new child to determine which classroom he or she would be best suited for. I checked in with him the morning of the screening, and, as with the pasta, this was new, and he was nervous.

This time, however, we had a story close at hand.

As we sat in the lobby waiting for them to call his name, I had him retell me the story of pasta night—right from the nervous beginning through to the joyful end. He talked about being afraid of not knowing what kind of pasta they would be serving—he even smirked slightly, picking up on the humor of the words as he spoke them. He told the story of the bouncy houses and that he could eat as much of his favorite pasta as he wanted. "And! They didn't even make me put meat on it . . . I could just eat it with butter and salt." He shot me a side-eye, realizing that he might have just busted himself. When I didn't seem to mind, he continued all the way to the end, and I watched his spirit lift as he got to the part about it actually being fun.

Just then, they called my son's name for his interview. He rose from his chair, smiled at me, and walked into the screening. Ten minutes later, he came out and bounced his way over to tell me just how fun it all had been.

That night before bed, I had him tell me both the story of pasta night and the story of kindergarten screening out loud in his own words, from beginning to end.

A few short weeks later, another big new experience loomed for my son, the poor guy. I could tell he was a little nervous like before, but when I asked him about it, his response delighted me. "This time," he said, "I feel nervous just like I did at pasta night and when I went to the kindergarten talk, but I know that new things can turn out to be fun."

It was a proud moment—evidence that a story had taken hold. I could have said to my son, "Don't worry. New things are fun!" and left it at that. If I wanted to take it up a notch, really reinforce the idea, I could have repeated it like a mantra every time he seemed frightened.

Instead, I told him stories that turned the abstract idea of "new things are fun" into something vivid, memorable, and concrete. Now, when my son encountered a new event, instead of fear triggering a response that held him back, he could retell one of the many stories of when new things were actually the best, thereby changing the way he approached a new situation altogether.

The lesson for parents—and anyone else interacting with kids—is that *equipping kids with statements isn't as powerful as equipping them with stories.*

Stories are memorable. They're sticky. They're emotionally charged. Each time you use stories, you're equipping kids with a tool they can use later on and expanding their ability to put things into perspective. You're helping them see that something that feels scary now is actually a small part of something much bigger.

With every story you tell a child, you build the scaffolding that frames how they see themselves and enables them to build their own yellow brick road.

THE ULTIMATE INHERITANCE—A STORY

I once had an older gentleman approach me after an event. He said he appreciated my message as it applied to his work, but he had another question.

"Should I tell stories to my grown children?" he asked. "They always seem so busy. They have kids and careers of their own . . . I don't even know if they're listening."

Rest assured, the stories you tell your kids don't just matter when they're young—they matter always. Tell stories to your kids during those awkward middle school years. Tell stories to your high schoolers—they might roll their eyes, or they might not even look up from their phone, but make no mistake, they're listening. Tell a story to your kid when they come home from college or the night before they get married.

Tell your children their stories, no matter how old they are. Each time you do, you reinforce the essence of who they are as people. Don't just tell them that they're resilient—tell them the story of their resilience. Don't just tell them they've always been curious—tell them the stories of their curiosity in action. Don't just tell them they're stronger than they think—tell them the story of a time you witnessed their unbelievable strength.

The stories from our youth are valuable long after the innocence of childhood has passed. Even if they look too busy for something as silly as a trip down memory lane, *tell them stories*. It's the greatest gift you can offer—the gift of perspective. The gift of watching someone grow and seeing them in a way they can't possibly see themselves.

MAKING SPACE FOR STORIES

Meet Lisa.

Lisa was struggling. She had signed up for the self-storytelling group, even though it was out of her comfort zone. And, as she expected, it was hard. She had difficulty finding both stories that served her *and* stories that held her back. She knew they were there, but for whatever reason, she couldn't seem to distill them and drag them into view where she could choose them or leave them behind.

By the end of our time together, Lisa had made some great progress and had made an equally important realization: she had never learned to tell a story.

Not in a formal sense—not a presentation or a pitch, but rather storytelling in the more natural way of sitting around and retelling an event to someone after it happens.

"My husband is a great storyteller," she said. "He starts telling a story at the dinner table, and all the kids just sit and stare and hang on every word. And then I start to tell a story, and I get a few words in, and everyone's eyes have glazed over."

Lisa wasn't upset about this, necessarily, but she had figured out something very important. "Growing up, my husband's family always sat around and told stories. He would get home from school and tell the stories of his day. He got a lot of practice." It was as if she had solved a mystery. Self-storytelling was hard for her because she was a *beginner*. She was a grown, accomplished woman but a brand-new storyteller.

As she shared that realization, something clicked for me.

My mother made me the storyteller I am.

She loved hearing my stories. I told her the crazy things that happened in my fourth-grade class. I told her the silly things Brian W. did in fifth grade. And I already told you about broomball. When the stories got more challenging in middle school, she was there for any of them I was willing to tell.

Weekends in high school, I competed on the speech team. Meets would last all day Saturday, and then Sunday morning, I would wake up, walk into the living room, and my mother would already be waiting on the couch, holding her coffee, waiting to hear the story. And not just high-level stuff; she wanted to hear every detail. We would sit there for *hours,* and my mother let me tell her the *whole* story. Even now, as a mother myself, I can still call my mom (my dad will join on speakerphone) and tell her every detail of every story that has happened.

It's wonderful to have a mother who will listen, but after my conversation with Lisa, I realized it was much more. These story sessions with my mother allowed me to tell my stories out loud (remember the strategies in chapter 7?), reinforcing the good ones and helping me to process the bad. Every one of those Sunday morning sessions was creating a storytelling habit that has given me a head start in overcoming doubt and breaking through barriers that keep me from where I want to be.

In encouraging and delighting in and taking the time to not only listen to my stories but to *want* to hear them, my mother gave me the opportunity to start collecting the bricks for the yellow brick road I would eventually begin to build.

And then I asked myself, do I do the same for *my* kids?

Do I give space for their stories?

Truthfully, I don't think I do. The pace of life is so fast. We're always going in different directions, even if we're not going any-where. Michael and I have a lot on our minds. The kids have homework and activities and friends. But after my time with Lisa, I realized I needed to *make* time and space for my kids to share their stories. Not just because I want to hear them, though I do, but because knowing what I know about the power of stories, I want them to start practicing *now.*

If you have children in your life, yours or not, ask to hear some of their stories. You may just change their future.

TELL THE STORY, CHANGE THE WORLD

When I started in my new role as Chief Storytelling Officer at *SUC-CESS* magazine, I was immediately thrust into the inner workings of publishing the next issue of the magazine—an issue that was already a few weeks behind. ("We were waiting for you to say yes!" they said.)

My first job was to choose ten phenomenal women to feature in the magazine that month. I would interview each of them for a new podcast I would now be hosting, as well as write their stories for a print piece in the magazine. And I would do this while my kids were going to school in our apartment, and I had to record podcast episodes via Zoom from my bedroom closet.

In other words, I had my work cut out for me. And I was thrilled. The list of women we put together was incredible, and I felt so honored to be able to have conversations with each of them.

There was one who was particularly special for me. It was the very first name that came to mind, the woman I wanted on the cover of the magazine, the incomparable Misty Copeland.

Misty is the first Black female principal dancer at the American Ballet Theater. When she said yes, I almost died. Not only because she's amazing, but because I knew I was earning ultimate mom points; my daughter *adores* Misty Copeland. A budding ballerina herself, she is in awe of Misty's power and grace. Every ad and article that features Misty stops my daughter in her tracks.

One warm, late June evening at the end of my daughter's first-grade year, I surprised her with tickets to *Swan Lake* where she could see, live with her own eyes for the very first time, Misty Copeland dance. We sat in the very back row in the theater at Lincoln Center, and though the show started *after* my daughter's bedtime and we had to leave at intermission, she sat on the edge of her seat, barely breathing, as she watched. Even a six-year-old could tell this woman was more exquisite than any book or article could articulate.

After the performance, dressed in a leotard and neon yellow ballerina skirt, my girl danced her way home through the New York City night, twirling and leaping down the sidewalk that had seemed to transform into her very own yellow brick road.

The interview from the closet went great. Misty joined from her Upper West Side apartment, fresh from a workout, her dark curls casually framing her face. She was as relaxed and graceful in conversation as she was on a stage.

She shared her story, and at the end, when I mentioned I had a ballerina who would be so honored to say hello, Misty kindly obliged. I called to my daughter, and within moments she bounded around the corner and into the closet. Her virtual ballet class was about to begin, so her hair was already tucked neatly into a tight bun atop her head.

She stared at the screen, and in the split second before nervously waving *hello* and telling Misty her name, I saw something flash across my daughter's face. It was the look of meeting your idol, the woman who is so magnificent, so glamorous, who sets a standard so desirable, it is completely unattainable. And then realizing: she looks like a normal girl.

A girl kind of like you.

Misty clearly has experience meeting starstruck ballerinas. Even through the inherent awkwardness of Zooming into a closet, she asked my daughter some ballerina-to-ballerina questions. Then we said our goodbyes, I turned off the lights I had hanging from the shelves, and I walked into the living room where my daughter was jumping around on the kind of high that is only possible from hearing your idol say your name.

"What did you think?" I asked.

"That was amazing!" she squealed.

"Yeah? She's pretty nice, isn't she?" I asked.

"Yes! So nice!" she squealed.

"Did anything surprise you about Misty?" I asked. She paused for a moment and turned her head slightly to the side, revealing her long, graceful neck.

"Well . . ." she started slowly, thoughtfully. As if she were working to sort through her thoughts and turn them into words. "She didn't look the way I thought she would."

And while one might assume that was a statement related to race—Misty as a barrier-breaking Black ballerina—it wasn't. My daughter knew Misty looked different than she did and that Misty's journey was different than her own. This was about Misty, without the gorgeous costumes and while sitting in her apartment across the park, was a normal girl . . . just like my daughter.

Yes, Misty is a superstar, but she is also a human. With human hopes and human struggles.

We talked, then, about how amazing ballerinas are also normal girls. They get sweaty from exercise; their curls come out of their buns. They work hard; they rest. They have friends and family and wear normal clothes. Then my budding ballerina bounded into her room to sign into her ballet class.

It was a brief moment, but its brevity made it no less important. A story was born that day. A story I have made note of in my own journal, and now here. A story for when the day comes and my daughter's comparisons are not as sweet, simple, or straightforward as admiring a bona fide superstar, but rather comparing herself to a classmate, or a colleague, or someone she follows on social media. A story for when she starts to wonder if they have something special that she doesn't have. A story for when she gets too wrapped up in others' highlight reels and forgets that backstage, or when Zooming in from their home, they're a normal girl, just like her.

And if *they* can do it, why not her?

Changing the world starts here. Imagine what would be possible if the next generation grew up fully equipped with stories to lift them when they felt down, to encourage them when they felt weak. Imagine what would be possible if the next generation's default wasn't to let the negative stories run rampant but rather the positive ones. Imagine if the next generation were equipped with stories of all the lessons they'd already learned and therefore didn't face spirals of doubt and unworthiness. We would have an entire generation of people who saw the light in themselves and could then, in turn, believe in the light of others. What a beautiful world it would be.

It's possible. But it has to start with you.

You have to tell it forward.

It's true that you can't go back and "rewrite" the past.

But you can start *now*.

You can find and craft and tell stories for your children. Stories for *other* children. And you can give the gift of story to other parents to help fill in the gaps and offer additional glimpses of who their kids truly are. You can listen and create wide-open spaces for their stories to be told and heard and, as a result, processed and solidified. For every story you capture and share in an effort to equip someone with stories that will serve them, you are doing your part to build a generation of people who, quite frankly, don't need this book. People who don't need instructions on how to choose better stories to live better lives because they'll already know how.

Because you showed them.

Through the stories you told.

13

THE EMERALD CITY

It's All Stories

We are not who we are because of our atoms, our
molecules, our DNA. We're who we are because of the
stories we tell ourselves—about the pain we're in, the hopes
we have, the dreams we live with.

—SETH GODIN

After the final curtain call of that fateful amateur production of *The Wizard of Oz*, my mother and I went to the lobby to greet the actors and have my program signed by the small-town celebrities.

To my delight, my mother knew the Scarecrow. He was probably a guy from church, but I was immensely impressed, and apparently, the feeling was mutual; he took one look at me in my blue- and white-checked dress, then crouched beside me and asked, "Do you want to meet Dorothy?"

My wide eyes and wondrous nod were a clear *yes*. He scooped me up and carried me off backstage.

I still remember the scratch of straw sticking from his costume as he carried me through the back hallways of the theater and down a stairwell. We stopped before a door labeled "Women's Dressing Room," where he raised his Scarecrow eyebrows at me, then knocked dramatically.

"*Dorothy*," he said in his most theatrical Scarecrow voice. "There is someone here who wants to meet you."

The door slowly opened revealing, none other than—

A nice young woman.

She didn't have flowing brown locks and blue bows; her hair was pulled up in a ponytail.

She wasn't wearing a blue- and white-checked dress like me; she wore jeans and a T-shirt.

No ruby-red slippers either; just a pair of sneakers.

The young woman looked at me. I looked to the Scarecrow, who, as if on cue, said, "Kindra, this is Dorothy."

She smiled and began engaging in some Dorothy-to-Dorothy chitchat. And the whole time she spoke, I remember looking at her as if I were solving the mystery of a lifetime.

You *are Dorothy?* I wanted to say. *You just look like a normal girl. Like me.*

I thought, *I could be you.*

A story was born that day.

At first, when I was a child, it was just the fun story of the day I got to meet the girl who dressed up as Dorothy.

As I've grown, it has become the story I tell myself when I feel the cloud of comparison creeping in or spot an iceberg of self-doubt on the horizon. Anytime I start to wonder if someone else has something that makes them special and leaves me lagging, I remember Dorothy.

Anytime I begin to think maybe I *can't*, I remember that once the dress and the shoes were put away, she was a normal girl, just like me.

———————

With all the wonder and splendor that is *The Wizard of Oz*, in all the mystique of flying monkeys and magic shoes, it's easy to forget some of the most important parts of the story.

Dorothy wound up in Oz because she ran away to escape her problems. She was looking for that perfect "somewhere over the rainbow." A place where things went the way she wanted. Where she didn't have to fear mean old neighbors or, as the story moved on, wicked witches.

But there are always fears. There will always be apple-throwing trees meant to discourage us or fields of flowers designed to put us to sleep. There will be billowing voices and final requests as impossible as securing the brooms of our enemies. And on more than one occasion, we will often find ourselves staring at an hourglass . . . wondering where the time has gone . . . and if there is enough left.

Make no mistake, there will always be writing across the sky beckoning us to surrender.

We cannot escape these fears.

What we *can* do . . . is choose what to do in the face of them.

We *can* choose the stories we tell ourselves.

Yes. *Changing your life is as simple as choosing better stories to tell yourself.*

That's it.

It's simple, yes, but not *easy.*

And therein lies the road ahead—the yellow brick road, you might say.

That road is made of stories. Each brick a different one, a distinct moment. And not all those stories are good. Not all are helpful. Not all *serve.*

Some of those bricks are handed to you. Some bricks are accidents. Some bricks come on the winds of fate, some wrapped in bad luck. The not-so-good stories are there . . .

But so are the good ones.

Many of the bricks *do* serve. Or *could*, if we let them. If we *chose* them. They are the bricks of good fortune, of golden opportunity. They are the bricks of kindness, and hope. They are bricks of challenges met, skills gained, and wisdom hard earned. They are the bricks of laughter, love, and joy. And though they may sometimes feel too small to matter, they are there.

We all have them.

We just have to seek them out.

No matter the brick, no matter the story, you get to *choose* how you see and place each one. You can build a yellow brick road that leads you across the gaps in life, or you can create one that leads you in circles.

The choice is yours.

And as for the Emerald City? I think we all need our own Emerald City. We all need to hope, and to dream. But remember what Dorothy found when she arrived there: the real magic was in the journey to reach it, not in the city itself. The real magic was in the stories.

In the end, the legendary Wizard himself was a story. And Dorothy's journey? That was a story, too.

It's all stories.

It is up to you to choose the good ones.

Kindra Hall
Spring 2021

If I ever go looking for my heart's desire again,
I won't look any further than my own backyard. Because if
it isn't there, I never really lost it to begin with.

—DOROTHY, *THE WIZARD OF OZ*

ACKNOWLEDGMENTS

The book process is an interesting one in that, on the one hand, it's a very solitary experience. I wrote many of these chapters alone in a house hours away from my family in a deserted town where I didn't see another human for days. On the other hand, a book requires a whole team, a community of people, and endless Zoom calls and emails and strategy sessions if there is any hope of the words being read, and I am so grateful for my team.

First, my family—Michael and my sweet kiddos. Thank you for giving me the space to write and celebrating with me along the way. If ever I need a story to help me believe in myself more, I need look no further than the three of you.

To the participants in my storytelling project, this book wouldn't be what it is without you. Thank you for courageously diving into the depths of yourselves and working so hard to find and change the stories you are telling yourself. Our time together remains one of the most fulfilling experiences of my life.

To those who read the early version of this book and offered your endorsements, thank you. Those words of encouragement from people I deeply admire and respect meant the world to me at that very vulnerable time.

My agent, Kathy Schneider. It's hard to believe it's been almost five years since our first conversation. So much has happened, so much has changed, and yet my gratitude for you never will. Thank you for everything you and the whole team at JRA, including Chris Prestia, Julianne Tinari and Hannah Strouth, do to share this message with the world.

I remember the morning I was on the phone with Dan Clements and we decided, just hours before you were supposed to be on a flight to New York City to meet in person about this book, to cancel the trip. We were pretty sure we were overreacting and at the very least, would meet a few weeks later . . . that was March 13, 2020. We still haven't had that in-person meeting, but that didn't slow us down. Thank you for helping me shape this project and get words on the page in such a creatively difficult time.

Even though I thanked you earlier, I wanted to say a very special thank you to my son, Arn Hall, for helping me with some of the research for the book. I'll never forget the afternoon you came into my bedroom with a sheet of research on rats in New York City, complete with sources. I was so proud and very grateful.

My editor, Tim Burgard. Thank you for believing in this project in such a big way and for all the calls and conversations to make it a piece of work I am so proud of. To Becky and the whole team at HarperCollins Leadership, I am so grateful to have you as a partner in these crazy times. And to Mark, Elena, and the team at FortierPR—thank you for making sure as many people as possible know this book exists.

To my internal team—Tiffany, Tori, Andrea. Thank you for helping me tell my story on stage and on social and for keeping my business running and my sanity intact (for the most part). Lauren and Paige of the SiSu Agency, thank you for all the things you did that I didn't even know needed to be done. And a big thank you to Shanna for handling third and fourth grade when the classroom was in our home instead of at a school so that I could write.

And lastly, thank you to my beloved friends and family who have encouraged me, supported me, and cheered me on. When I need to choose a better story, the best ones usually have you in it.

NOTES

Chapter 1

1. Michelle Scalise Sugiyama, "The Forager Oral Tradition and the Evolution of Prolonged Juvenility," *Frontiers in Psychology* 2 (2011), https://doi.org/10.3389/fpsyg.2011.00133.

2. Polly W. Wiessner, "Embers of Society Firelight Talk Among the Ju/'hoansi Bushmen," *Proceedings of the National Academy of Sciences* 111, no. 39 (September 2014): 14027–14035, https://doi.org/10.1073/pnas.1404212111.

3. D. Smith et al., "Cooperation and the Evolution of Hunter-Gatherer Storytelling," *Nature Communications* 8 (2017), https://doi.org/10.1038/s41467-017-02036-8.

4. B. Geurts, "Making Sense of Self Talk," *Review of Philosophy and Psychology* 9 (2018): 271–85, https://doi.org/10.1007/s13164-017-0375-y; Amy Morin, C. Duhnych, and F. Racy, "Self-reported Inner Speech Use in University Students," *Applied Cognitive Psychology* 32 (2018): 376–82, https://doi.org/10.1002/acp.3404.

Chapter 2

1. P. J. Zak, "Why Inspiring Stories Make Us React: The Neuroscience of Narrative," *Cerebrum* 2015, no. 2 (2015).

2. Brian Boyd, *On the Origin of Stories: Evolution, Cognition, and Fiction* (Cambridge, MA: Harvard University Press, 2009).

3. Michael Kosfeld et al., "Oxytocin Increases Trust in Humans," *Nature* 435, no. 7042 (2005): 673–76, https://doi.org/10.1038/nature03701.

4. Julio González et al., "Reading 'Cinnamon' Activates Olfactory Brain Regions," *NeuroImage* 32, no. 2 (May 2006): 906–12, https://doi.org/10.1016/j.neuroimage.2006.03.037.

5. Véronique Boulenger et al., "Subliminal Display of Action Words Interferes with Motor Planning: A Combined EEG and Kinematic Study," *Journal of Physiology-Paris* 102, nos. 1–3 (2008) 130–36, https://doi.org/10.1016/j.jphysparis.2008.03.015.

6. Simon Lacey, Randall Stilla, and K. Sathian, "Metaphorically Feeling: Comprehending Textural Metaphors Activates Somatosensory Cortex," *Brain and Language* 120, no. 3 (2012) , 416–21, https://doi.org/10.1016/j.bandl.2011.12.016.

7. Aimee Groth, "The Mental Strategies Michael Phelps Uses to Dominate the Competition," *Business Insider*, June 16, 2012.

8. R. Rosenthal and L. Jacobson, "Pygmalion in the Classroom," *Urban Review* 3 (1968): 16–20.

9. P. D. Blanck et al., "Measure of the Judge: An Empirically-Based Framework for Exploring Trial Judges' Behavior," *Iowa Law Review* 75, no. 3 (1990): 653–84.

10. David Keith Fitzhugh, "Pygmalion in the Athletic Training Room: A Qualitative Case Study Approach" (PhD diss., University of Tennessee, 2004).

11. L. A. Learman et al., "Pygmalion in the Nursing Home: The Effects of Caregiver Expectations on Patient Outcomes," *Journal of the American Geriatrics Society* 38 no. 7 (1990): 797–803, https://doi.org/10.1111/j.1532-5415.1990.tb01472.x.

12. Dov Eden, "Leadership and Expectations: Pygmalion Effects and Other Self-fulfilling Prophecies in Organizations," *Leadership Quarterly* 3, no. 4 (1992): 271–305, https://doi.org/10.1016/1048-9843(92)90018-B.

13. A. Vaish, T. Grossmann, and A. Woodward, "Not All Emotions Are Created Equal: The Negativity Bias in Social-Emotional Development," *Psychological Bulletin* 134, no. 3 (2008): 383–403, https://doi.org/10.1037/0033-2909.134.3.383.

14. A. M. Paul, "Your Brain on Fiction," *New York Times*, Sunday Review section, March 17, 2012.

Chapter 3

1. Stephanie Yang, "New York Rats Emboldened by Lockdowns Have a New Enemy: Sundrop," *Wall Street Journal*, July 27, 2020.

2. Melanie Gray and Dean Balsamini, "Giant New York Rats Overtaking Central Park and the UWS," *New York Post*, November 21, 2020.

Chapter 4

1. "How Large Was the Iceberg That Sunk the *Titanic*?" The Navigation Center of Excellence, US Department of Homeland Security, https://www.navcen.uscg.gov/?pageName=iipHowLargeWasTheIcebergThatSankTheTITANIC.

2. "Ninety Percent of an Iceberg Is Below the Waterline," USGS image, https://www.usgs.gov/media/images/ninety-percent-iceberg-below-waterline.

3. OnePoll survey for Wrangler, December 2016.

4. J. C. Norcross and D. J. Vangarelli, "The Resolution Solution: Longitudinal Examination of New Year's Change Attempts," *Journal of Substance Abuse* 1, no. 2 (1988–1989): 127–34, https://doi.org/10.1016/s0899-3289(88)80016-6.

5. The Conference Board, *The Job Satisfaction Survey*, 2014.

Chapter 5

1. R. Yehuda et al., "Holocaust Exposure Induced Intergenerational Effects on FKBP5 Methylation," *Biological Psychiatry* 80, no. 5 (September 1, 2016): 372–80, https://doi.org/10.1016/j.biopsych.2015.08.005; B. Dias and K. Ressler, "Parental Olfactory Experience Influences Behavior and Neural Structure in Subsequent Generations," *Nature Neuroscience* 17 (2014): 89–96, https://doi.org/10.1038/nn.3594.

2. Amy Morin, *The Verywell Mind Podcast*, March 1, 2021.

Chapter 7

1. "Matthew McConaughey—The Power of 'No, Thank You,' Key Life Lessons, 30+ Years of Diary Notes, and The Art of Catching Greenlights," *The Tim Ferriss Show*, Episode 474, October 19, 2020.

2. K. M. Krpan et al., "An Everyday Activity as a Treatment for Depression: The Benefits of Expressive Writing for People Diagnosed with Major Depressive Disorder," *Journal of Affective Disorders* 150, no. 3 (September 2013): 1148–51, https://doi.org/10.1016/j.jad.2013.05.065; A. N. Niles et al., "Randomized Controlled Trial of Expressive Writing for Psychological and Physical Health: The Moderating Role of Emotional Expressivity," *Anxiety Stress Coping* 27, no. 1 (2014): 1–17, https://doi.org/10.1080/10615806.2013.802308.

3. P. A. Mueller and D. M. Oppenheimer, "The Pen Is Mightier Than the Keyboard: Advantages of Longhand over Laptop Note Taking," *Psychological Science* 25, no. 6 (2014): 1159–68, https://doi.org/10.1177/0956797614524581.

4. G. Lupyan and D. Swingley, "Self-directed Speech Affects Visual Search Performance," *Quarterly Journal of Experimental Psychology* 65, no. 6 (2012): 1068–85, https://doi.org/10.1080/17470218.2011.647039; E. Kross et al., "Self-talk as a Regulatory Mechanism: How You Do It Matters," *Journal of Personality and Social Psychology* 106, no. 2 (February 2014): 304–24, https://doi.org/10.1037/a0035173.

5. S. Milne, S. Orbell, and P. Sheeran, "Combining Motivational and Volitional Interventions to Promote Exercise Participation: Protection Motivation Theory and Implementation Intentions," *British Journal of Health Psychology* 7, no. 2 (May 2002): 163–84, https://doi.org/10.1348/135910702169420.

Chapter 8

1. "How to Explain Gaps in Your Employment Record," Cutting Edge, October 16, 2020, https://cuttingedgepr.com/how-to-explain-gaps-in-your-employment-record/.

2. G. Oettingen and D. Mayer, "The Motivating Function of Thinking About the Future: Expectations Versus Fantasies," *Journal of Personality and Social Psychology* 83, no. 5 (2002): 1198–1212, https://doi.org/10.1037/0022-3514.83.5.1198.

3. Lisa D. Ordóñez, Maurice E. Schweitzer, Adam D. Galinsky, and Max H. Bazerman, "Goals Gone Wild: The Systematic Side Effects of Overprescribing Goal Setting," *Academy of Management Perspectives* 23, no. 1 (2009): 6–16, https://doi.org/10.5465/amp.2009.37007999.

4. Michael Shayne Gary, Miles M. Yang, Philip W. Yetton, and John D. Sterman, "Stretch Goals and the Distribution of Organizational Performance," *Organization Science* 28, no. 3 (2017): 395–410, https://doi.org/10.1287/orsc.2017.1131.

5. "Ryan Lochte," Wikipedia, https://en.wikipedia.org/wiki/Ryan_Lochte.

6. "How Do You Define Success?" *SUCCESS Stories with Kindra Hall* podcast, April 13, 2020, https://open.spotify.com/episode/6JgH0C6aBvF6BkBIHLK4qq?si=029145f7a5d54b55.

INDEX

ABOUT THE AUTHOR

Kindra Hall is the author of the *Wall Street Journal* bestseller *Stories that Stick*, which Forbes said "may be the most valuable business book you read." Hall served as the chief storytelling officer and contributing editor of *Success* magazine. She is internationally known for her expertise, research, and keynote presentations on the power of storytelling in business and in life.

Kindra lives in Manhattan with her husband, son, daughter, and their vizsla named Spacedog.

More resources can be found at
www.chooseyourstorychangeyourlife.com/resources